THE LIVING CHURCH BOOKS

Christianity today is confronted by such challenges that all Christians need to be well informed about the truths, strengths and enjoyments which are theirs in their heritage. They need to know, too, about the many experiments and reassessments which are renewing the Church for its mission in the contemporary world. Our aim in the Living Church Books is to contribute to the intensive educational effort which the crisis demands.

Titles already published

Agenda for Anglicans

DEWI MORGAN

Rector of St Bride's, Fleet Street, London,
formerly Editorial Secretary,
Society for the Propagation of the Gospel

WITH A PREFACE BY

Bishop Stephen Bayne

Executive Officer of the
Anglican Communion

SCM PRESS LTD
BLOOMSBURY STREET LONDON

First Published 1963

© Dewi Morgan 1963

Published simultaneously by SCM Press Ltd., London
and Morehouse-Barlow Co., New York

Printed in Great Britain by
Charles Birchall & Sons Ltd
Liverpool and London

CONTENTS

PREFACE

by the Executive Officer of the Anglican Communion

I CAN think of at least three good reasons why I should not have written a Preface to this book. One is that such a commendation, from one so profoundly involved in what the book is about, might be a kiss of death. May I say at once that *Agenda for Anglicans* is not an 'official' book? It reflects no party line, nor is there one in these matters; we do not have any company religion in the Anglican Communion; and my warm liking for this book is entirely personal.

The second reason is that it might seem unfair to single out this book for some special recognition not given to the other books by Anglicans about the Anglican Communion which are also in our minds. There are not many of these, to be sure, but they have come from the pens of most able and powerful writers, and I have no feeling that what Dewi Morgan writes has some unique claim on our attention not shared by Bishop Higgins or Bishop Neill or Bishop Wand or Canon Herklots or Canon Johnson (to name the five writers who have taught me most, in recent years, about our Communion). I could answer (and it would be true) that I would have written a public commendation for any of the others with equal pleasure. I wasn't asked to, so I didn't.

A third reason is that it is clearly indelicate for me to praise a book which quotes some of my words. There is no escape from this; it is indelicate; and the only excuse is my own intolerable wordiness.

But despite the sensible cautions, I still want to say publicly that I welcome this book and hope it will be widely read and equally widely pondered by Anglicans and others. I do so for three more good reasons.

First, *Agenda for Anglicans* helps us, very directly and plainly, to see the tensions and contradictions within the Anglican Communion. The chapters on 'Confessionalism' or 'The Administration of Mission', for example, plunge the reader into the practical issues, the daily stresses and the pulling and hauling, which are not only characteristic of Anglican life at this point, but are the issues which must be faced and resolved, if we are to be honestly and fully obedient to our vocation.

I said above that there is no party line among Anglicans about such issues. Indeed there is not. I do not agree with Mr Morgan, for example, in some of the things he says about missionary societies. He does not disguise his own preference, generally, for the 'society principle' as over against the 'unitary principle'. In this he is entirely within his rights; and so am I in not feeling such general acceptance of the 'society principle'. But the point is precisely here; this is a present tension within the Anglican Communion and a most important one. It is not, I think, a contest in which one or the other system must ultimately win. I do not doubt, myself, that each has a good deal to learn from the other and to teach the other. I long to have American Churchmen, for instance, as involved, personally and individually, in prayer and support, with the Church's mission overseas as is often characteristic of their opposite numbers in the Church of England. Equally do I long to see the day come in England when there will be some way for the united and total obedience of the Church of England to be manifested (as contrasted with the particular and voluntary and sometimes even partisan response which often seems to make obedience to mission an option for the more spectacularly devout or sentimental).

If there is to be the kind of dialogue which will permit each to learn from the other, there must be a way for us to be plunged into the tensions themselves; and I think *Agenda for Anglicans* helps to do that, as much as any brief book can.

Second, Mr Morgan has a rare skill at helping us to see the diversities of our Anglican life. As I wander around the Anglican world I grow increasingly aware of the need for precisely this knowledge of one another and our individualities. It is quite a different thing to be a member or a clergyman of the Church of England, say, than it is to be an Episcopalian in the United States. And there are equal or even more marked differences among the other churches of the Anglican Communion. And it is not good for us to stay imprisoned in our own provincialisms. A priest or layman from one church who swaggers around the world judging other Anglicans by what he has and is and can take for granted—such a person violates brotherhood at every turn, and condemns himself as well as others to even further divisons within Christ's Body (and heaven knows we have enough).

There is no one right way to be an Anglican. There is no Anglican church which is 'right'. The unity we have—deep and unfailing as it is—is a unity which lives and bears its generous fruit in diversity. And it is precisely this sense of unity in diversity which runs all through what Mr Morgan writes.

It should be added that there is more to this than simply knowing our diversities. There must go with the knowledge of them a necessary modesty of mind which permits us to accept them. Mr Morgan does not dwell on this spiritual need as a central part of our agenda—not as much, I think, as I should have done. I must confess that I grow daily more amazed at the sheer possibility of unity in Christ, despite and through and because of the differences among us; yet as I marvel at that, I marvel also at the childlike modesty which we must bring to the meeting with others, and the readiness to let them be themselves. This is part of our agenda, no doubt.

Finally, I am glad that Mr Morgan presents us with a picture of Anglican life which is unfinished—full of possibilities, of great hopes, of glorious promise of truth and grace—yet equally something which must continually be fought for. It is never ours to hold and treasure; it points continually beyond itself to something greater. If we were content to be simply one denomination of Christians among many, with our own peculiar tradition and ways, it would be no great thing to be an Anglican. All that would be required would be a measure of discrimination, to supply valid reasons for choosing this way of being a Christian over some other way.

In fact it is quite otherwise than this, at the heart of our life. There one finds no placid acceptance of the status quo, no easy comfort with ourselves and our incomparable liturgies, and all the rest of it. The vocation of an Anglican is inescapably and sometimes painfully and always profoundly ecumenical. We are driven by our own deepest insights and gifts into the fight to find and manifest an unimaginable unity, a unity already given us in the wonderful and terrible unities of God's creation and loving redemption of us, which has never fully been grasped and held by men.

Rightly he speaks of our duty to be faithful stewards of what God has entrusted to us. But to say this alone could be no more than a cheap justification of disunity. The other side of it is to see—as he does see—the fact that the truer we are to what we are and to what we have, the more certainly we are driven into ecumenical action, to seek the flowering and harvest, in unity with all Christians, of the unbelievably great seeds of unity planted in us, in Holy Scripture and creeds, in ministry and sacrament. For this awareness of the unfinished nature of Anglicanism, of the travail and hope which is inextricably interwoven with our stewardship, I must say that I am most grateful.

STEPHEN F. BAYNE, Jr.

AUTHOR'S FOREWORD

OF ALL the relationships between men, none calls for the thought, prayer and action of Christians more than what we have come to call the ecumenical movement. Outstandingly the most exciting mark of our century, this movement has reached what some would regard as a critical stage. It cannot stand still. It must either go forward or it must become a tantalizing dream of what might have been.

It is my conviction that if Anglicans are to be obedient to the call of God to unity and are to be active partners in its pursuit, they must examine their treasures, if any. Just what do they have to bring in return for the gifts they will receive from other Churches?

Far too few Anglicans are asking that question. And they unhappily align themselves with the man who had but one talent and left it unused.

What use has God for the Anglican Communion? Why has this curious family of some forty million Anglican Christians, spread across the world, come into being? What, if anything, gives it an identity? Can it define any of its own strengths and weaknesses and, if so, can it do anything about them?

This book has been constrained into being by a conviction that not enough people are asking such questions as those. The author readily acknowledges his incompetence to provide the answers. He merely hopes that he can stimulate others more able and at the same time begin to crystallize that divine discontent with itself that Anglicanism must always feel.

The careless reader may construe some parts of this book as an implicit criticism of other Christian bodies. To do so would be entirely alien to the author's intentions and harmful to all the hopes for the coming Great Church that true Anglicans must ever formulate in prayer and demonstrate in action. This is not a book about what other Christians are *not* but an attempt to see what Anglicans are.

Perhaps there is not a single original thought in this book. But then, neither is there in Anglicanism. For Anglicanism claims no proprietary right to any private theological castle.

One personal note should be added, if only to exonerate the Church of England. My childhood, youth and the whole of my parochial ministry were spent in the Church in Wales, a dis-established Province which, sometimes overshadowed by its English sister, has both motive and opportunity for looking at the physical home of Anglicanism with what it hopes is an objective eye. For the last twelve years I have lived in England in body but have had a constant necessity to rove round the whole Anglican Communion and beyond in mind and, I hope, in spirit. To attempt to attribute any of this book's deficiencies to the outlook of any particular Province of our Communion would therefore be unfortunate and unfair. For such deficiencies I must accept personal responsibility. But for any virtues the book may have I gladly refer the reader to the books, letters, reports and wise words of people across the world.

My indebtedness to others will be obvious and my inability to make acknowledgements manifest. But one act of recognition must be recorded. It is to the Missionary Society of the Anglican Church in Canada. It was the deep privilege of an invitation to lecture to a seminar in London, Ontario, which proved the final stimulus to put down on paper thoughts which for years had clamoured inside me for expression but which, aware of a sense of my own incompetence, I had so often decided to leave to others more capable.

There comes a time in every man's life when he has to try to assess his resources and see what more he can do to help others. The same must be true for a Christian Communion. Here is the beginning of an attempt on the part of one who is truly thankful he is an Anglican because he believes that through Anglicanism, God will help him to become something more.

I

Authority and Freedom

IT IS only the non-Christian who can cherish the illusion that Christian commitment means a peaceful existence where all problems are solved and all the mental agonies removed by a formula which can be found if you turn up the right page of the right book. For the outsider the image of the Church is all too often one of a body which has satisfied itself (and probably nobody else) that it has the answer to all intellectual ponderings and all moral dilemmas. The answer may be wrong. The answer is probably a negative prohibition or a facile assumption. But answer it is and the Church, the outsider alleges, is complacent about it. The outsider betrays his mind every time he complains that the Church has given no detailed directive in some situation. 'If Jesus Christ had been alive today, I don't know which side he would have been on but he would have been on *someone's*' is the sort of letter you see in a popular newspaper. And only rarely does anyone point out that what Jesus gives is a statement of principle, not a detailed easy-to-follow set of rules like a cookery recipe. 'Yes,' said Jesus when asked about taxes, 'it is right to give Caesar what is actually his.' But he did not absolve the enquirer from further thought about the nature of Caesar and his rights. The sort of commands Jesus gave were positive and demanding—in more than one sense. 'Be ye holy' presents us with a challenge, not a simplified do-it-yourself kit. When the Church gives detailed directions on any contemporary problem it has to ask itself if it still resembles its Master.

The more committed a Christian becomes the more he realizes that one thing God keeps asking of him is the sacrifice of a straining, questing mind as well as a contrite heart. How can it be otherwise when we are concerned with a God who is infinite? With a God who emptied himself and then men killed him? How can there be any intellectual rest about a faith which calls a felon's death on a cross a beautiful thing?

The Christian life, mentally, is a long safari through an unknown land of paradoxes, each of which produces its own trauma. Humanity, seeking to be at ease in its own Zion, inevitably rebels against this constant pilgrimage. It is so much easier to be settled, so much more gratifying to be the sort of person who has 'arrived'. Court shoes are easier on the feet than pilgrims' boots and, somehow, so much more respectable. But respectability may have little to do with one who was born in a stable, had nowhere to lay his head, kept company with sinners and finally put away the last shreds of status symbols when he went out beyond the city wall to die the way he did.

The Christian life is to be a life of struggle. And if, as we believe, the Anglican life aims to be a truly Christian life, then the Anglican must be identifiable more by his wound scars than by his war medals. For he, more than most, finds his way strewn with paradoxes and they are the sort of paradoxes which do not readily dissolve into easy and comforting formulae. They remain obstinate, brain-bruising paradoxes.

At the moment we are particularly concerned with the tension between freedom and authority. Does the Anglican have either? Or does he live in a curious half light where he must put up with chaos where he seeks freedom and mere temporizing and smooth words where he seeks the paternal assurance of authority?

The Anglican tradition, says Archbishop Lord Fisher,[1] is unique in Christendom. We are called to attempt the hardest

---

[1] *The Archbishop Speaks*, ed. E. Carpenter (1958), p. 91.

of all tasks in the Christian Church. It is comparatively easy to stand for order and institutionalism and authoritarianism. It is comparatively easy to stand for complete freedom of the spirit and liberty of action. It is attractive and simple to walk with those who are altogether of the same mind. It is far harder and requires higher qualities of Christian insight and dedication to seek to keep in a right relation divergent ideas which, though all within the circle of loyalty to Christ, yet contradict each other sharply.

Anglicans, says Lord Fisher, are called to a hard task. The image of Anglicanism as a sort of ecclesiastical muddling through, consonant with the image of the Englishman, is false. Anglicans *are called*. They are under authority, and the Anglican Church is a more authoritative body than some of its own members realize. Yet to affix such a label can be profoundly misleading. For freedom, as well as authority, is the desire of this Church. How can we reconcile such apparent antitheses?

When an Anglican comes up against a hard question his first instinct is to turn to his Prayer Book which he knows will lead him back to the Bible. Has the Prayer Book any relevance to this question?

There are many points in this Book where we might send down a probe, but one of them particularly seems to crystallize a meaning in this context. It is the Marriage Service. And marriage, we may remember, signifies 'unto us the mystical union that is betwixt Christ and his Church'.

'Wilt thou have this Woman ... and, forsaking all other, keep thee only unto her?' the officiant solemnly asks. The man replies, then the woman faces the same question. Separately, as individuals, they make an act of supreme self-limitation. Gone forever is the freedom to look round and choose a mate. A great unscalable wall has been built round one whole area—a vital, God-given area—of human life.

The freedom is cast away and each submits to the authority

of the other. Yet, having submitted, a new freedom is promptly granted, and it arises directly from the loss of the first. 'I N. take thee N. to my wedded wife, to have and to hold . . .'

To *have* . . . and to *hold*. The circular ring which slips on a finger symbolizes, for both man and woman, a whole body given away into the authority of another, and yet in the same moment receiving the complete freedom of possession of the body of another. And together they receive the freedom, God's freedom, to *make* (the word is surely significant) love, and to seek participation with God in the freedom he has given to humans to make new souls. Freedom can conceive no greater freedom. Yet it is all one with an authority, indeed a mastership, over the body of another. Human language was deeply discerning when it decided a paramour must be called a mistress. For he who takes the body of another inevitably gives away his own, even if it is just the artificial, ephemeral giving of a lustful moment in a squalid city backstreet.

Freedom and authority. How far have we advanced our discussion? Not very far, perhaps. Except that we have discovered that they are not two separate, disparate, mutually exclusive entities. They cannot, in this life, exist in any pure form in isolation. You cannot analyse a series of factors in any situation and say: 'Lo, we now have freedom and nothing but freedom, or, authority and nothing but authority.' The bits which go to make up a human existence cannot be taken apart and examined quietly and critically. We can look at life only in the arena of living. And it is an arena subject to a million constantly changing factors.

Freedom and authority. We can too easily reach a state of bemusement where we assume that each of these words has a valid, absolute meaning of its own. And we can too easily beguile ourselves with the belief that either can be pursued, or is worth pursuing, in isolation. Can you, by any stretch of the imagination, define the life of God Incarnate as a life of freedom? He put away his freedom when he emptied himself. And in putting away his freedom he exposed himself to the tyranny of Satan in the Temptations, to the will of a corrupt High Priest and a petty Roman civil servant.

Can you, by any stretch of the imagination, suggest that his life on earth was a life of authority? Not if by authority you mean what we humans want it to mean, the power and capacity to *make* men do things, believe things, be things. For his authority, too, he put away when he emptied himself.

It is true that he said: 'Full authority . . . has been committed to me' (Matt. 28. 18: N.E.B.). It is true that observers said he taught as one having authority. But his own words emphasize freedom much more: 'Who made me a judge over you?' And his greatest parable of fatherhood depicted a son who had the freedom to be as prodigal as he would.

Christ, who was among men as one who serves, did not come to earth to model either freedom or authority in the human categories of those words. He came to show God who is the only ultimate authority and God in whose service is the only ultimate freedom.

St Paul understood all this so well. In no circumstances would he let his Gentile converts come under the authority of the Jewish Law. He kept on insisting on the contrast between law and faith. And any follower of his who showed a tendency to embrace the Law was roundly accused of being false to his liberty in Christ. As far as Paul was concerned the Law was what engendered pride. A law is something which *can* be obeyed in every jot and tittle, and luxurious is the sense of self-satisfaction which accrues. But you do not earn salvation by attention to every clause of some contract with God. Salvation is something you can only accept as a free gift. And accepting a free gift calls for humility.

The Bible is much more a book about liberty than a book about law, about freedom rather than about authority.

Yet the history of Christ's Body on earth, the Church, has been a long succession of lurches from pole to pole, of lunges from freedom to authority and from authority to freedom.

Bishop Bayne has drawn a sharp picture of ecclesiastical authoritarianism gone sour : [1]

> I do not think clericalism was a prerogative of the Middle Ages; all that one can say about the clericalist of medieval times was that he could make a better living at it than his twentieth-century counterpart can do. But the emotional and psychological returns of clericalism are identical in every age, and the clericalist is the same in every age. He suspects everybody, even God. He understands his duty as that of protecting his flock. He worries for fear they may hear dangerous opinions; he is alarmed lest they be called on to make decisions for which they are not adequately prepared. He guides them and guards them and hovers over them like a hen over her chicks; and most of all, he refuses to let them be free and mature and responsible people who have something to say to him and something to do with him. The clericalist will work like a mad-man; he will be the most assiduous and devoted of pastors; he will wear himself out shepherding his people; he will teach and teach, and preach and preach; he will love them to death; he will do everything for them except let them grow up.

Such is authoritarianism. And equally unwelcome is the type who has become so intoxicated with freedom that he has to obey its every whim. At which point he must say with the Gospel demoniac into whom many devils had entered: 'My name is Legion.'

Both authority and freedom have their own built-in dangers. Yet Church history is a story of lurches from one to the other one. Are we to see these things as mere chance staggerings? Or as the inevitable pendulum swinging from an authority which made freedom seem the greatest desideratum to a freedom which made authority the deepest yearning? Or as the divine dialectic being worked out by God, who shows his purpose through the variegated screen of human history?

If the last is indeed the truth then surely we cannot expect

[1] *Enter with Joy* (1962), p. 108.

the consummation of this dialectic until the consummation of history. Until then we must expect the impediments to the true marriage of freedom and authority to be more visible than the marriage itself.

In the Anglican Communion such impediments are indeed visible. Painfully and persistently visible. So visible that men often cannot but regard them as a scandal, a foolishness, a stumbling block—especially those men who believe they have found either true freedom or true authority.

Our twentieth century with its conflicts and disorders, its restlessness and its very real fears, is a day when men appear to long for the security which lies in submission to authority. 'I am bewildered—do my thinking for me' is the agonized chorus which wells up, and the totalitarian State is the result. With a totalitarian Church not far behind it. We err if we suspect this means a straight reference to the Roman Church. In the new era of Pope John XXIII, it is probably a much less true inference of Rome than it is of the sects which flourish on the very excess of the demand they make on their adherents. Fundamentalism in the use—or rather the misuse—of the Bible is much more amorphous and therefore much more insidious than a Decree of Infallibility. But they both demonstrate the same thing. There is a deep desire, especially evident in the contemporary world, for authority, either to possess it or, if that is not possible, to have it exercised over one. Almost as if the only choice before humans was to be either a drug-peddler or a drug-addict. Is there no escape from narcotics altogether? *Must* authority be available?

The Anglican says that totalitarian authority is not only unnecessary, it is evil. And so we stand both with and apart from extremes. A distinguished scholar has made this comment on the Church of England in the seventeenth century:

In their repudiation of the Roman efforts to cover her dog-matic innovations under the authority of tradition, and in their insistence on the Bible as the sole final criterion of orthodoxy, the Anglicans stood with the Protestants; but on the other side they departed from the Reformers of the Continent and from the Puritans at home in their rejection of what they regarded as an illegitimate extension of Scriptural authority ... It was a question of fundamentals and accessories. Certain inferences from the central dogma of the Incarnation they allowed as self-evident, even in a way as essential to the faith that saves; but they hesitated over, and with the passing of time drew back more resolutely from, the doctrines of absolute predestination, effectual calling, justification by faith alone, imputed righteousness, and the whole scaffolding of rationalized theology which Luther and Calvin had constructed about the central truth out of an unbalanced exposition of isolated texts. Not that way lay the simplicity of the faith. Also, and even more unhesitatingly, they followed Hooker in his protest against the Puritan denunciation of all the accessories of ritual and discipline for which specific warrant could not be found in Scripture. Here they stood with Rome in so far as they would admit the immense value of tradition in much that was vital to religious observance, though it might not be necessary to salvation.[1]

Anglicans avoid the extremes of authority. But they also avoid the extremes of the so called free thinkers whose life becomes an unravelled sackcloth of conflicting desires and impulses. Anglicans avoid extremes but that does not mean a smooth passage.

It is relatively easy to accept a rigid totalitarianism which has no loose ends and relatively easy to meander on accepting nothing at all. But Anglicans are called to a harder path. To quote the Bishop of Chester, Dr Gerald Ellison:[2]

To be an Anglican requires many qualities which even some men of the highest religious genius have lacked. It requires the courage to apply the individual conscience to the challenge of the Faith; it needs the patience to wait till the answer to some problem not yet obvious is revealed, and the honesty on occasions to say 'I don't know'. It needs the

[1] *Anglicanism*, ed. P. E. More and F. L. Cross (1935), p. xxvii.
[2] *The Anglican Communion* (1906), p. 84.

love to be tolerant with those whom we think misguided or foolish in their expression of their opinions. It needs the self-discipline to accept the demands of our Faith, not because we are told we must do so but because we believe such things to be true. Here is the true genius of Anglicanism and it is very precious.

Commenting on this passage, Bishop J. W. C. Wand says: 'It may be that Anglicanism demands something that not a great many even of its own members can give consistently. Perhaps the atmosphere is a little too rarefied, the tone pitched a little too high, for truly popular appeal.'[1]

Bishop Wand is amongst the most scholarly and most experienced of Church leaders. His statement is cautious and carefully qualified. For Anglicanism seems all the time to be reaching for a fullness of truth which lies always beyond its finger-tips: a fullness which seems to hover round this juxtaposition of freedom and authority.

William Temple has made a similar point in respect of Christian behaviour:

This Anglican way is an extraordinarily difficult one to follow. But it is difficult with the difficulty of an ideal. Christian character consists of a balance of many virtues, any one of which is comparatively easy to achieve without the others, just as, in the signal instance of the Pharisees in the Gospel, it is tolerably easy to set a high standard of conduct if you do not make much effort to be sympathetic with those who fall below it. Or it is easy to be sympathetic with those who fall below it if you do not maintain a high standard. But it is overwhelmingly difficult both to maintain a high standard and also to show sympathy with those who fall below it; and this is the way of Christ.

That kind of difficulty is inherent in the way of any ideal and supremely so of the Christian ideal, and that kind of difficulty in our Anglican mission is itself some evidence that our feet are on the right path. Don't let us suppose that

[1] *Anglicanism in History and Today* (1962), p. 240.

because, in the face of that difficulty, there is an amount of disunion among us sometimes, which is not equally apparent in other Communions which are adopting a method to my mind demonstrably less ideal, therefore the Church of England is a feeble body or a body tending towards its own disruption. We are steadily going forwards in the effort to do what is as difficult as anything can be—the holding together of different sides of a truth so rich that no individual and no group ever appropriates it fully. Moreover, we hold out, as is commonly said, a hand both to the ancient Churches of the East and to Rome on the one side, and to all those who with us are heirs of the Reformation on the other; and in that we have a position unique in Christendom, the full value of which can only be realized for the universal Church so far as we are true to both sides of our tradition.

And so I would say, do not fear parties. They will arise; they ought to arise. We shall none of us grasp the whole richness of the Gospel as the Church of England has understood it and is learning more fully to understand it. And, of course, we shall act most easily and most effectively in combination with those whose angle of vision is much the same as our own. So groups will spring up and there will be parties. We do not fear parties but we do fear partisanship—we do fear, that is, the spirit which tends to think of the other groups in our one Church as anything other than comrades and allies. We fear anything which leads us to regard them as our opponents. What we seek to possess in fuller measure even than now is the unity of friends of different opinions and temperaments who, because of their diversity, are able to enrich each other.[1]

What William Temple is saying is that the moral standards of the Church are as authoritative as its doctrine as expressed in the Creeds. But the great Anglican assumption is always that the Church is dealing with grown up men and women who can be trusted to make their own offering of themselves and fulfil their own responsibilities, needing only the chance to

[1]*Essays in Christian Politics* (1927), p. 205.

refer to authority as they wish. The Anglican may see through
a glass darkly, but he is not to be spoken to as a child in the
over-simplified *fiats* which are all a child can understand. He
is old enough for mature, responsible—and dangerous—conscious participation. He is not a dictator's pawn nor a cipher
in a totalitarian state.

Indissolubly connected with the totalitarianism of either
extreme, of course, is the whole concept of infallibility. This is
as much a mark of the biblical fundamentalist as of any supporter of the Vatican. And it is entirely alien to the Anglican
mind which holds that infallibility is an attribute of God alone.
He has given us the truths necessary to salvation. But in his
mercy he has made them few in number. And, above all, the
Truth he has given is a Person not a catena of propositions.
And that Truth at once carried all authority and yet promised
his members all freedom.

It is an authority which surpasses anything which stems from
a priori ideas of infallibility. And it is a freedom which facilitates the growth into the utter fullness of truth. This is no
diminished faith. But neither is it a prison-house.

Freedom and authority. The more we try to analyse them as
disparate entities the more bewildered we get. And that is inevitable. For God himself has built them together into a more
intimate and intricate system of checks and balances than even
the American Constitution.

Now the good American knows he has three duties in respect
of that Constitution: (1) to understand it, (2) to see it operates
as effectively as possible, (3) to help to get it improved in any
way possible.

Good Anglicans can do no less with their constitutionless
Communion. So where is wisdom to be found? Where is the
place of understanding?

God himself provides the answer in the person of Jesus Christ.
How did he demonstrate the authority of God in the flesh of
man? In the first place it is worth noting in passing that the
more real authority anyone has the less he has to assert that

authority. Jesus certainly did little to assert authority. The most
obvious fact of all his ministry was that he did nothing
to compel belief. He did nothing to force upon men what he
was saying or what he was. Rather he left it to appeal to the
reason and conscience of men. One might go further. Much of
Jesus' ministry simply was not teaching in the sense of a school-
master retailing facts for a pupil to soak up as a mere act of
receptivity. 'He that hath ears to hear, let him hear.' At
times one almost feels that Jesus was on the verge of being
indifferent as to whether men listened or not. Such a false
impression, of course, is immediately corrected when one
remembers what he was prepared to suffer, and did indeed
suffer, in order to proclaim the truth. But the abiding realization from studying Jesus' methods and his use of his authority
is of love using love's ways in an intense conviction that no
other methods would do.

Jesus never imposed the truth on anyone. Even more, Jesus
never even offered the truth without, so to speak, writing into
the transaction a clause 'subject to your *actively*, not passively,
receiving it'. At all times he encouraged, called for, a response
from his hearers. And the response asked for was that men
should relate what he said to their own experience and verify it
by all the other things that life had taught them.

Thus did Jesus show his respect for the human personality.
He was not there to manipulate it or to dominate it. He was
no hidden persuader using subliminal methods. He was there
to fulfil personality, not destroy it. And fulfilment calls for
active response. All Jesus' teaching, therefore, was in the fullest
sense of the word, communication, a sharing. Jesus spoke and at
once referred his words to his hearer's conscience, reason and
experience.

Such communication is the duty of his Church on two levels
or in two stages. In the first place the Church has ever to ponder
its Master's words anew and refer them to its own corporate
conscience, reason and experience. Having formulated the result
the Church must corporately speak and refer its words to the

conscience, reason and experience of all those who are not yet its members. And both of these are, and must remain, unfinished tasks.

Now the question which concerns us in this book is, what is the relevance of such things to the Anglican Communion? In commending the Faith to those outside the fold it would surely seem an advantage to proclaim as concise a body of beliefs as possible. Anglicanism secures this by distinguishing between fundamentals and accessories. There are those things which are necessary to salvation and they are fundamental and there are those things which are convenient in practice. They are accessories and may well be flexible. The fundamentals can be reduced to the scope of the Creeds, backed always by Scripture and Tradition. Anglicanism therefore needs no long and detailed manifesto, and of all the world-wide Christian bodies it is probably the one with the least formulated and defined demands upon its adherents. Which means, surely, that it is the one most open to the possibility of relating what God in Christ said to the infinite variety of conscience, reason and experience of the multitude of the nations, and therefore the one with the greatest hope of eventually reaching the richest expression of the Faith. As the body with the greatest potential for completeness—a completeness involving all the varied human ingredients—it is the one most capable of speaking to the greatest variety of men, and therefore the one carrying the heaviest of all missionary responsibility, though Anglicans are lamentably unaware of the fact and certainly fall short of their vocation. This does not mean that the Anglican hope is that all the world should be Anglican. But rather that Anglicans have a particular share in the responsibility of all Christendom to help the world to become Christian. Anglicans must always look through Anglicanism to something greater.[1]

Have we perhaps left behind the Anglican Communion as it is and moved on to an Anglican Communion as we would

---

[1] See e.g. the international symposium on *The Mission of the Anglican Communion*, ed. E. R. Morgan and R. Lloyd (1948).

like it to be? Have we left the reality panting heavily somewhere in the rear? Indeed we have. The Anglican Communion
still has to shed many things—the over-obtrusive shreds of its
Anglo-Saxon cocoon, for example—before it is capable, or
worthy, of its future.[1] But unless we dare to keep in our mind
some pattern of that future we may easily lose interest. We
must firmly remind ourselves that our primary concern is not
with the past of our Communion nor even with its immediate
present. Our job is to keep asking God to show us what sort of
a future he wants for it, and in the light of that to ask him
what is the next step he wants us to take.

The concept of all the nations actively responding to God's
word in Christ by relating it to their own conscience, reason
and experience is surely one which carries any Christian mind
into very green and lush pastures. We have in the past deprived
ourselves of much vision and encouragement by not relating
this idea to all our missionary work.

The real reason for such missionary work, we must keep
reminding ourselves, is the glory of God. But there are many
ancillary reasons which must surely give pleasure to God as
well as enrichment to ourselves. One of them is especially
relevant here. It is the fact that Englishmen, Africans, Chinese,
American, whatever, *are* different. They all have a conscience
fulfilling the same function and they all have powers of
reasoning working on the same lines. But the raw material of
their own particular experiences and ancestral memories are
different. When, therefore, they come to look at the same
problem they respond with, at least, different emphases,
different half-lights. When all those emphases and half-lights
are added together the sum total is infinitely richer than any
one of its constituent parts. The missionary, therefore, who
takes Christ to a Japanese is hoping that when that Asiatic
has responded by relating Christ to his own conscience, reason
and experience he can give the missionary something more

[1] See e.g. *Essays in Anglican Self-Criticism*, ed. D. M. Paton (1958).

than the missionary gave in the first place. We have so impoverished our Christ by making him a European gentleman. And we have so caught ourselves in the mesh of our own limitations that we need the Japanese, the Eskimos, the Polynesians, the whole world, to help us escape. Thus, in a very literal sense, do we magnify Christ by taking him to the nations.[1]

How does all this reflect on the authority and freedom of the Church? The answer, surely, is obvious. If the Anglican Communion attempted at this moment to spell out a fully comprehensive, detached and finally binding statement of the Faith it would do little more than demonstrate that it had not yet asked all the questions, let alone heard all the answers. Yet any statement which lacks the adjectives 'fully comprehensive, detailed and finally binding' cannot be denoted authoritative in the fullest sense of the word.

We without them cannot be made perfect. Joseph, speaking to his corn-seeking brothers a long time ago, yearned to see Benjamin. 'Except your brother be with you,' he said, 'ye shall not see my face.' And except they saw his face and had his favour they would get no food. God is saying just that to all the human race. 'Except your brother, all your brothers, be with you, you shall not see my face.' Except our brothers have joined us and have shared with us their insights, the glass through which we see God is more opaque than ever. And seeing God's face, tracing the lineaments of God's being, is the duty and desire of a Christian.

Scattered round the oceans and continents of the world there are some forty million Anglicans. If someone could assemble all that they separately know about God in Christ, through the response of their own conscience, reason and experience to his Word, then all would know much more corporately than they would ever do individually. And the more they know the nearer they would be to gaining a true authority. And,

[1] See the discussion by Canon H. G. G. Herklots of the spiritual results of the growth of the Anglican Communion, in *Frontiers of the Church* (1961).

curiously enough, at the same time gaining a true freedom.

But is there anything practical to be said? How is the Anglican Communion to assemble all those loose ends and bind them into one volume? The nearest we get to it at the moment is a Lambeth Conference. But this has at least three limitations—it meets only once in ten years, it lasts only about six weeks and it is limited to bishops only. And future Lambeth Conferences are likely to carry more and more problems—if it is only the language troubles of men who represent every major race grouping in the world.

The Lambeth Conference, consistent with its Anglican nature, has never claimed for itself any authority beyond the moral authority of its members. No Lambeth resolution has any binding quality in any province or diocese until it has been accepted by the appropriate authority of that province or diocese. Perhaps it is just there that its future value lies. It certainly provides the Holy Spirit with room to operate. But the Holy Spirit has never told men to abhor the administrative, organizational flair which seems to be the characteristic of North Atlantic man. Is God calling us at this moment to take a further step forward towards linking more closely the branches of the Anglican family and so pooling their scattered wisdom? I make no claim to inside information in this matter. But it does seem that there are some relatively simple steps which could be taken.

Perhaps it is too sudden a shock for a chapter like this to produce a practical suggestion. But it at least gives the author a chance of relieving his mind of something which has nagged for years. Why do we not have a great compendium of theology compiled by Anglican authors who are specially well placed to write on various subjects? Perhaps compendium is the wrong word. What we need far more is a dialogue, a continuing conversation. The problem is just how such a conversation can be brought into being and sustained with sufficient liveliness and regularity to make it fruitful. Perhaps we are not yet ready for that (though we dare not assume that without close investigation). But a compendium is surely an immediate and practical proposition. And how invaluable it would be, especially, perhaps, for those parts which came from the 'younger' Churches which have so much to tell their older brethren. For example, the western world with its at least superficial Christian permeation is constantly asking just what is Christian conversion. In a semi-Christian (I deplore the word post-Christian) society the chasm between Christian and non-Christian is concealed by an infinite gradualness. But for a Christian living in a pagan society the differentiation is sharp, and such a Christian ought to be able to tell Westerners a very great deal of what changes are involved when a man accepts Christ. Again, the whole doctrine of Christian marriage has become blurred for Western man. How much a Christian living in, say, a Muslim society could tell him about the differences between monogamy and polygamy !

The very fact that such questions can be asked asserts that Anglicanism has no equivalent of what delighted the Medes and Persians (and encompassed their downfall?). But it also asserts—and this is much more important—that Anglicanism has the potential for moving towards a theology richly studded with gems from the mines of many Solomons. It will have a depth and splendour quite beyond the imagination of those who are heirs of a single European culture. 'The leaves of the tree were for the healing of the nations,' said St John the Divine. And the healing of the nations will be for the fulfilment of the tree.

It is such a vision of all nations giving and receiving which seems so desirable and yet so tantalizingly remote in a fragmented world. Now let us make no mistake, such an interflow of life between the splintered groups of man will be the gift of God and not the prize of our own merely human endeavour. Yet in making his gift God calls for our hands. For as St Theresa told us long ago, God has no other hands but ours. The realization of this vision, then, is not to be accomplished by a little folding of the hands and a little sleep. We are called to

active participation, the participation of sons hastening about
their father's business. And that means the participation has
to be intelligent as well as active. All the time we must
be driving ourselves back on all the truth we can find.

For Anglicans this means the whole corpus of doctrine, not
as it was reshaped by some sixteenth century religious society,
but as it was given to the Apostles and worked out by the
Fathers. And the Anglican is offered the *whole* of this communication. It is ineluctably a package deal. He is not invited
to make from it such selections as provide a comfortable
spiritual anthology, but to wrestle with the immensities which
constitute so uncomfortable a spiritual agony. The Anglican
Communion has realized, however dimly, that to struggle thus
demands freedom—the freedom to make a mistake, many mistakes, as well as the freedom to choose aright. Unless you are
free to go wrong, going right has no moral value. The Church
does not have to worry too much about honest error, for
it knows that God can put all things right. And the Church
knows that the error of the lover is more acceptable than the
most precise accuracy of the indifferent.

Unless you have to make stark intellectual choices you are
not being educated. The best in you is not being led out. This
matter of education does not depend on an I.Q. It just depends
on getting out the best that is in you. It is one of the
cases where you are required to pursue the course (with all the
effort that word 'pursue' evokes), rather than to pass examina-
tions. It is the sort of wonderland where dreams come true
and everyone who runs in the race can have the prize.

The Anglican Communion believes in education, not direction. It has a respect for the freedom of the individual which
it can have learned only from God. So it gives the individual
a choice. Those who see such things from the outside assume
therefore that Anglicanism has no mind of its own. So when
Anglicans find themselves in conference with other Christians
they hear the charge: 'You have no theology.' Insofar as the
accuser (that is far too harsh a word for any present-day con-

ference of Christians, but we will keep the metaphor unmixed) means there is no specifically Anglican theology, he is right. There are no special Anglican doctrines. For Anglicans there are only all the doctrines of the Catholic Faith as they are found in Scripture, summarized in the Creeds and set forth in the General Councils of the undivided Church. These find their formulation in the Prayer Book or, at least, in the principles the Prayer Book seeks to enshrine.

There is no Anglican theology yet there is something which is specifically Anglican. When two Anglicans who in their own circles would be held to represent wide differences of churchmanship are in conference with other Christians, it is the things they have in common which are most obvious and most memorable. This perhaps is because they approach their problems in the same way—something which stems from what might be called an Anglican attitude or an Anglican atmosphere. When they or others try to define the strange something in common the usual result is a spate of high-sounding words which do little more than darken counsel.

Anglicanism refuses to be reduced to words. But, then, so does the Holy Spirit. He blows where he chooses. And perhaps he finds the Anglican barque of some particular use as its sails fill with his gentle wind.

A sailing ship seems a very good symbol of something which responds both to freedom and authority. Unlike a railway engine, subject to the steel authority of the rails, it can change its direction. And yet it acknowledges its need of an authoritative wind to fill its sails.

Anglicans do acknowledge and accept authority. But they also remember that Christ gives the truth which shall make men free. Those who are growing to the fullness of Christ's stature are constantly discovering new depths in the God whose *service* is perfect *freedom*.

2

Regional and National Churches

GENERALIZATIONS SEEM to come in two kinds. Or perhaps it is truer to say that generalizations have two different effects on different sorts of people. They may be a narcotic tranquillizing the mind against further effort, a soothing balm which says, 'Think no more, here is the final truth.' They may, on the other hand, have all the violence of a grenade suddenly exploding among a somnolent people, shattering the peace of prejudices and preconceptions and forcing them back on to their intellectual haunches.

In his book *Christendom*[1] Dr Einar Molland makes a sweeping generalization which belongs securely to the second category—especially since Dr Molland is not an Anglican:

> If selection were to be made of a particular doctrine as specially characteristic of the Anglican Communion as a whole, it would certainly be the theology of the Incarnation. While other Churches emphasize the Resurrection of Christ or the Atonement, the Anglican Communion regards the Incarnation, the doctrine of the Son of God made man for us men and for our salvation, as the central theme of Christian theology. If the Orthodox Church is 'the Church of Easter', or the Lutheran 'the Church of Good Friday', the Anglican Church may be described as 'the Church of Christmas'.

Only a page or so before Dr Molland has described the Anglican Communion as 'the most elastic Church in Christen-

[1](1959), p. 148.

dom'. So he is certainly not now suggesting that the Anglican Church is so rigidly 'Incarnational' in its thinking that it forgets the other great acts of God in man. But there is much real substance in what he says and his argument can be supported not only from looking at characteristically Anglican theologians but also by looking at the emphasis of the Anglican Liturgy. Our point for the moment, however, is not to argue Dr Molland's case but to accept it is a premiss and see where it takes us.

The essence of the Incarnation is not that God loved man so much that he had an all powerful desire to be somewhere vaguely near him, to be somehow vaguely identified with him. The doctrine of the Incarnation says starkly that at a given time in a given place, accepting all the given limitations of that given situation, God became a particular Man. He did not, primarily, become some undefined man in general or symbolize the essence of humanity but he became the man Jesus of Nazareth about whom historical writers could write historically.

There was a moment when the God-Man was solely a Jew looking back through his mother to an identifiable Jewish ancestry. He was not a Persian or a Greek or a Roman but a Jew. Salvation was indeed of the Jews. We may well ponder with W. N. Ewer:

> How odd
> Of God
> To choose
> The Jews.

It may seem odd to us, who like comfortable generalities, that God should be so particular as to choose even the best-prepared of the world's peoples for his purpose. But the fact remains: He did. And since it is one of God's facts it is bound to have a meaning for us and that meaning is not merely a historical remembrance but also a present relevance.

Is there any connection between the particularity of the

Incarnation and the emphasis which the Anglican Communion lays upon national or regional Churches?

One reason why the Anglican Communion can never become a 'Confession' in the accepted connotation of that bit of contemporary jargon is because of its insistence on the integrity of these national Churches. As far back as the very first moment when the Anglican Communion (as opposed to the Church of England) could have taken the road to confessionalism—the first Lambeth Conference—the safeguards seem to have been written in. For on the agenda of that conference was 'Intercommunion between the Churches of the Anglican Communion'.

You don't start talking about *Inter*communion when you are dealing with a single confession or denomination. Subsequent Lambeth Conferences have returned with diligent regularity to this subject with expressions such as:

> There are two prevailing types of ecclesiastical organization ... centralized government and ... regional autonomy within one fellowship. Of the former, the Church of Rome is the great historical example. It is upon the latter principle that the Anglican Communion is founded. It is a fellowship of Churches historically associated with the British Isles. While these Churches preserve apostolic doctrine and order they are independent in their self-government, and are growing up freely on their own soil and in their own environment as integral parts of the Church Universal. It is after this fashion that the characteristic endowment of each family of the human race may be consecrated, and so make its special contribution to the Kingdom of God. The bond which holds us together is spiritual.[1]

The freedom of each member Church to express its opinion and to expect all others to respect its opinion is, clearly, a mark of the Anglican Communion. It is one of its most striking aspects and one in which it bears in its body the marks of the Reformation and those who fought that freedom and private

[1] Lambeth Conference, 1930, *Report*, p. 153.

judgement might be respected. The spirit which in the political context gave rise to democracies has a spiritual counterpart in Anglicanism, which is one reason why Anglicanism may have a particular vocation in this dictator-ridden century.

The emphasis on national Churches, of course, is not an Anglican invention. It is shared by other Churches and, notably, by the great body of Orthodox Christians. But the Anglican Communion seems to give it a greater significance than most—to the degree that it is constantly talking of it as a desired goal for all.

> We desire to set before our people a view of what, if it be the will of God, may come to pass. As Anglicans we believe that God has entrusted to us in our Communion not only the Catholic faith, but a special service to render to the whole Church. Reunion of any part of our Communion with other denominations in its own area must make the resulting Church no longer simply Anglican, but something more comprehensive. There would be, in every country where there now exists the Anglican Church and others separated from it, a united Church, Catholic and Evangelical, but no longer in the limiting sense of the word Anglican. The Anglican Communion would be merged in a much larger Communion of National or Regional Churches, in full communion with one another.

Thus spoke the bishops at the 1948 Lambeth Conference.[1] Just what does the Anglican Communion mean by National Churches? Does it mean that one becomes a member of the Church by the mere fact of birth and that re-birth and Baptism should become superfluous? Jesus talked about going out into highways and byways and compelling them to come in, but surely any possibility that a man should be forced into Church membership simply because he has been born is in every way alien to what Jesus said, did, was. To imagine that a National Church is one of which everybody entitled to a certain sort of

[1]*Report*, p. 122.

passport is necessarily a member is to betray the lurking pre-occupation of churchmen with the question: how can we fill our churches? How can we get the queues outside the lychgate and thus prove what a good show we are running? The moment we begin from such a standpoint we caricature the essence of our Faith. For the Church is the Body of Christ who came to minister. The function of the Church is not to ensure its own congregational corpulence. And the function of a National Church is not to have a membership identical with the civil census list but to be among that nation as he who is the Servant.

That means a National Church must be identified with its nation but cannot, until the perfection and consummation at least, become identical with that nation. The National Church must become incarnate in that nation, but only in the same way as God became incarnate in man and at the same time stood in judgement on man; so the National Church must stand apart from (the essence of holiness) that nation. It must therefore not become equated with any mere nationalism nor must it accept traditional patterns of national life simply because they are the traditional patterns of that nation. The Church must be able to agonize over all the problems of its nation but it cannot always rejoice over all that that nation regards as its joys.

We are, semantically, in a difficult region. For the sum total of what most nations regard as their joys is the raw material of which nationalism is made and nationalism is among the most dangerously sensitized words in the language. Perhaps it would be as well if we distinguished between nationalism as the explosive force and nationality as the sum total of the God-given characteristics of a nation.

Although the metaphor can easily be strained into error, there is nevertheless a major truth in saying that the Church must be the conscience of a nation. And conscience is an intensely personal possession. There is a real sense in which a nation must *possess* its Church as mankind *possessed* God when

God gave his Son into the human species. Yet God's Son was never the prisoner of humanity, even at the moment when he stood before Pilate or the High Priest. And the Church must never become the prisoner of its nation—like a conscience which has been shackled into submission. In this, as in all other things, the Church must remember whose Mystical Body it is and ponder his nature. It was when he most of all demonstrated how much he had handed himself over to men—by letting them kill him—that he also most demonstrated that he was not their prisoner. He could use even a gallows as an instrument of victory. So, too, the Church must give itself over into the hands of its nation. But by the very moral stature it derives from its Lord it must tower over its nation. As the salt becomes one with the other ingredients in bread, the Church must be part of its nation but it must never lose its savour. And like the yeast it must not lose its dynamism.

The first function of any National Church is to be the channel through which God's love is shown to that nation. And since God has made the nations different we may presume he has different ways of showing his love to them—subject always to the one eternal and universal way of giving his Son to the end that all that believe in him might be saved.

The Church of India, Pakistan, Burma and Ceylon succeeded in crystallizing something of that when it wrote in the Preface to its Constitution: 'When the legal connection formed by Acts of Parliament[1] between the Church of England and the Church in India was removed, the Church of India, (Pakistan), Burma and Ceylon gained the rightful freedom of a regional Church within the universal Church to direct its own life and bear its own responsibilities. This Church aims at accomplishing for India, (Pakistan), Burma and Ceylon what the Church of England has accomplished for England. As the Church of England, receiving Catholic Christianity from the Undivided Church, has given a characteristically English interpretation of

[1] It is worth remembering that the Anglican Church in India had its autonomy before the State did.

it, so the Church of India, (Pakistan), Burma and Ceylon aspires to give a characteristically national interpretation of that same common faith and life.'

'A characteristically national interpretation.' Those words are explosive. They suggest many things and not least the possibility that a National Church may exist for *other* nations. We must come back to that but first we must worry out a little further the idea of a National Church within its own nation.

First of all, it is not an invention of the Anglican Communion or even of the Orthodox Churches. It begins in the Bible where its *locus classicus* is 'John, to the seven Churches of Asia . . .' And if one may draw any lesson from the second and third chapters of the Revelation of St John the Divine, it is the fact that each of those Churches has 'a characteristically national interpretation'.

Before leaving this point for the moment, we quote Archbishop Philip Carrington speaking at Minneapolis in 1954. He is an authority on the ancient Church.

It was in such a way that the greater apostolic centres of Christianity acquired, in primitive times, a position of influence and prestige. Constitutional definition did not occur until much later. If the Anglican Communion has failed to provide an efficient and central authority of inter-provincial character, it only reflects the condition of the Primitive Church itself after the destruction of Jerusalem. The apostolic mission, which had been the creation of the Lord himself, had by then imparted itself to the churches of the Dispersion. (And I might pause over that word. Perhaps the Anglican Communion is a Diaspora.) The apostolic mission was now vested in the episcopal order, and distributed throughout the whole world. Everywhere it organized itself in the local form of the diocese. The association of these dioceses into larger families appears remarkably early. We find regional councils being held as early as the time of Ignatius.[1]

[1] *Anglican Congress Report* (1954), p. 45.

The second point is that a National Church must never be 'the spirit of nationalism: religious division'.

As we have already implied, there is perhaps no more lethal word in our day than nationalism. It has, usually rightly, been held responsible for all the international griefs we suffer. But we are on more than debatable ground if we argue that something is in itself sinful simply because men have been able to make it an occasion of sin. Christians who criticize nationalism forget that their own Old Testament (and sometimes the New) is among the most nationalistic books ever written. Is there anywhere in literature a more poignant expression of nationalism than the Exile psalms?

'The nation,' said Lambeth 1958, 'like the family, is part of God's ordering of human life.' Christians are not against the nation any more than they are against fathers and mothers and children being a family unit. But what Christians are against is that distortion of a nation which is so sin-producing a characteristic of fallen humanity today. Nationalism can be a creative thing, for nationalism can and should be a positive love for your own nation, and love is always creative. But love, too, can be twisted into an excessive, arrogant and aggressive pride and then it is sin. But no National Church, having its mind firmly rooted upon God, can ever be proud of its own nation. The more a National Church fulfils the true nationalism of *loving* its own nation the more it is bound to be aware of the nation's need for grace. The more the National Church sees the vision of God, the more aware it will be that its nation exists not for its own sake, but for the sake of God and, therefore, for the sake of all other nations. By definition, then, a National Church exists for the National Churches of all other nations. Each National Church is to be a Servant Church and all together are to be servants of God.

The National Church, then, will see its functions as pointing its own nation to God, cleansing what is impure and unworthy in that nation and strengthening what is good and pure.

But it has never been the function of a National Church to

live out its life in splendid isolation inside its own national
frontiers. That was not possible for the Seven Churches of Asia
when the Apocalypse was being written, nor was it possible
for Christendom, even in a day when the peoples of the world
were so much more stationary in their own backyards. It
certaintly is not possible in a day when satellites squeeze the
world into a neighbourhood and every race wanders restlessly
across the face of the earth. Nationalism in the old, limiting,
negative sense is even more impossible than political isola-
tionism. No Church can go it alone. That has always been true.
Nowadays it is also obvious.

The Anglican Communion has always realized all this however unconsciously. The indifference of eighteenth century
England to the Anglican Mission in general, and to Anglican
growth in North America in particular, can never be anything
less than a scandal. Yet deep among the obscure motives for
that indifference may have been some dim recognition that too
much detailed care about other nations' growth could easily
topple over into interference.

Any implication there that we hold a brief for Anglican
indifference is unwarranted. But we might find some further
clue about how God the Spirit works through man, by looking
at 'indifference' more carefully.

The Church of England has always had towards its daughter
Churches something of the attitude of the Head of the Secret
Service in thrillers who says to his agents: 'You must remember
we cannot help you. If you succeed you will get no recognition.
If you fail we must not be involved. You are on your own. Good
luck, my boy.'

That paragraph is not a casual brush-off for the quite
stupendous Anglican missionary work done from England. It
is just a tear-shedding for how much more could have been done.
It may also be a reflection on the fact that the *Church of
England as such* has never done any missionary work. It has
left it all to the private enterprise of its missionary societies.
The whole Anglican Communion is, humanly speaking, the

result of the endeavours of groups of dedicated individuals who got together and tried to persuade the rest of the Church to get alongside them.

What we have today is a series of independent, grown-up, Anglican Churches across the world. And they are all different. Perhaps it is a law of nature that all children are different. Every mother seems convinced that her children hardly resemble each other. God obviously means every individual to be different. Does he have a similar attitude about Anglican Churches—and, beyond them, about National Churches?

The more you talk to members of different parts of the Anglican Communion the more you are reminded of the conversational gambit of most parish priests. 'Of course, my parish is different. We have unusual problems here.' Sometimes they protest it so loudly that one is led to suspect they seek an excuse for something which will not match up to standards. But they may be right.

Certainly there are major differences between the Province of Canterbury with centuries of history and what the real estate agent would call 'a matured garden', and the Province of Uganda and Ruanda-Urundi still in the toddler stage; or, between the Church in exuberant America and the Church in immemorial India.

Once upon a time, wrote Bishop Ernest Burgmann of Australia, nearly all Englishmen in Australia belonged to the Church of England; nearly all Irishmen were Roman Catholics; nearly all Scotsmen were Presbyterians . . . The English in Australia assumed an effortless superiority, which the Scots resented and the Irish hated. The Scots worked with head and hand and prospered, the Irish decided to rule the country and went into politics. The English tended to trust in the strength of their ruling-class traditions to keep them on top in the Australian scene. The Church of England in Australia shared this confident sentiment. It remained reserved, respectable, complacent, and reposed. Religious emotion was the preserve of the Methodists. Some small sects also added variety to the religious scene, but Anglicans were not impressed ... Anglicans have rested on their oars too long and their privileged position is a thing of the past.[1]

'Ruling-class traditions to keep them on top ... confident sentiment ... privileged position.' Anglican readers in Asia, in Africa, in South America, in so many places, will wonder if those words are about the Communion to which they belong.

But so will a member of the Anglican Church in Canada wonder if he is a fellow-member with one who belongs to the Holy *Catholic* Church in Japan or the *Protestant* Episcopal Church of the United States of America. The very variety of names of individual Churches in this Anglican Communion could be construed as pointing to chaos unlimited. Yet, from those names we can learn a lot, not only about some other Church but also about ourselves.

The first Church to get its name was the American and it happened in 1789. The one title which made Americans reach for their guns at that time was Church of *England* or anything implying it. So there came into being that cumbrous 'Protestant Episcopal' and Americans have been arguing about it ever since and the debate continues. (It looks as if it still has enough stamina to reach the General Convention agenda for some years to come.)

But let's pause for a moment to look at the circumstances of the naming ceremony. America was a *pot-pourri* of the nations. They had come in numbers large and small from their homelands and brought their religious affiliations with them. Accordingly, no Church could be *the* Church, as was the case in England, especially as the fathers of the new nation had decided Church and State must be separated. Each Church had to be a private society The last sign of the Anglican Church in America having anything remotely resembling a 'ruling-class tradition', such as Bishop Burgmann laments in Australia, was the fact that two-thirds of those who signed the Declaration of Independence were Anglicans and George Washington walked

[1]*Anglican World*, vol. 1, No. 2, p. 7.

across the road and received the Holy Communion in an Anglican church immediately after being sworn in.

Not least because of its history, the Protestant Episcopal Church in the U.S.A. has many valuable lessons to teach the other Churches of the Anglican Communion, lessons which would possibly have been lost if there was a world-wide Anglican Church, instead of a world-wide Anglican Communion of Churches.

Perhaps the currently most obvious lesson for the Church in England arises from the utter dependence of the Protestant Episcopal Church on its people's generosity. As a result came all that was germinated in the U.S.A., cultivated in other places such as Australia and now flowers in England as the stewardship movement. Undoubtedly it is important. But it is not the only contribution which the Protestant Episcopal Church may make to the Anglican Communion . . . or even the most important.

When a man is ordained an Anglican priest he is not ordained in deepest fact as a priest of the Church of England or the Church in Korea or wherever. He is ordained as a priest of the Church of God and accepts no limiting terms such as 'Anglican'. The same applies when a bishop is consecrated.

There is a vital and relevant lesson to be learned here, and it is one which may be lost in a welter of other associations. In most parts of the Anglican Communion when a priest is ordained he makes vows of obedience to his bishop, and when bishops are consecrated they make their vows to their Metropolitan. Not so in the United States, for there both priests and bishops 'promise conformity and obedience to the Doctrine, Discipline and Worship of the Protestant Episcopal Church of the United States of America'. What lies behind this is the belief that it is the whole life of the Church to which Americans promise to conform, not simply the incarnation of the Church in any individual bishop or archbishop.

There is in that an idea of the wholeness of the Church which is important. It is this same idea of the wholeness which lies behind the fact that American overseas missionary dioceses are held to be constituent parts of the Church in the United States.

Here, so some would think, is a striking example of the way each National Church can and should learn from each other. The Church of England, for example, has something to learn from the American idea of wholeness as this applies to the universality of the priesthood and episcopate. It would then cease to tolerate such stupid bits of Erastianism as the Colonial Clergy Act. But it may also be possible that the American idea of wholeness has much to learn from the Church of England when it comes to letting an adult missionary diocese build its own nest away from the parent rookery. American Churchmen, so many think, show a form of ecclesiastical imperialism which is fascinating in people who were the first to take serious issue with British political imperialism. An ecclesiastical Boston tea-party in some remote corner might provide absorbing copy for newshounds of the world.

The fact that American priests take their canonical vows to the whole Church and not to their bishops might suggest that the American bishop was in some ways a lesser person than his counterpart in other places. But a close examination seems to suggest that there is a greater gap between bishops and the rest of the diocesan clergy in America than there is in England. (This is certainly not to suggest that American bishops are standoffish stuffed shirts; the very opposite is the case. Gaiterless and without 'palaces' they usually bowl an Englishman over with their approachability.) In England the offices of Dean of a Cathedral, of Archdeacon, of Canon, of Rural Dean all have their own status and together make a series of links between the leader of a diocese and the newest curate. In the United States such offices mean much less.

On the other hand, the laity in the United States mean much more—though (constant astonishment in a land of women so emancipated) 'laity' in many parts of American church government, notably in the General Convention, is apparently of the male sex only. Thus, the Vestry in the American Church is a much more powerful body than the Parochial Church Council in England. It is the Vestry, for example, which chooses a new incumbent and invites him to be their leader. And the laity (men only, we repeat) have a great deal of say in the General Convention.

There is, of course, historic reason for this. The American Church had no bishops until 1784, and so ideas of really democratic rule had a chance to root themselves before there could be much opposition to them. For a hundred years and more before that, and for long after that, the American Church suffered a paucity of clergy. There were not enough to go round, so parishes were, of necessity, often without an incumbent. And the people who had to run the show on their own could not then be relegated to a passenger seat when a priest was available.

It is all so different from the English story, where, for centuries, an incumbent seemed to arrive in an English village direct from heaven above, and usually appeared to bring with him the fruits of past endowments—which absolved the laity of the need to do anything to help him, and appeared to deprive them of the right to do anything to advise him.

There are other points in the American Church—its national organization, its struggle for identification, and so on—which equip it to say much to the Church of England. But we must not wander into a mere comparison of the Protestant Episcopal Church and the Church of England. The American Church has been chosen as an example simply because it highlights differences, good and bad, which in one way or another exist between all Anglican Churches.

In one sense, the American Church is a misleading example for it is so merged into an Anglo-Saxon background. In many Anglican areas that Anglo-Saxon background is rapidly disappearing and, in some, it has barely ever appeared. The Book of Common Prayer has become 'native', at least as far as translation goes, among the peoples of some 170 languages. There are more native Anglicans in Africa than there are in America. Nevertheless, the Anglican Church in America does provide an example for comparison and contrast with the Church of England.

Now there is something which must be emphasized. The points at which the American Church is different from the Church of England were not deliberately produced. There was no master plan behind them. They grew largely out of the practical necessities of a given situation. That is not a bad thing but it is rarely a tidy thing.

Our talk of Anglican Churches can too easily lead to an idea of a series of more or less identical households of God. If that fallacy becomes part of our mental furniture, it presents a barrier to our being able to learn from each other—and that learning from each other is so vital an ingredient of our Anglican opportunity.

There is real advantage in the fact that Anglican Churches are different from each other. But more impressive is what they have in common. The Preface to the first American Prayer Book, 1789, affirms that it will 'appear that this Church is far from intending to depart from the Church of England in any essential point of doctrine, discipline or worship; or further than local circumstances require'. Anyone from England who has been lucky enough to enjoy the warm hospitality of the American Church will know how he finds himself immediately at home. No acclimatization is needed. The differences do not begin to appear until later. But when they do appear they say something of importance and it is an importance which deserves to be shared.

It is tempting here to go off into a sermon on the need for the sort of communication in the Anglican world which would enable the Anglican world to benefit from all its varied insights. That is an ever-present headache and urgently requires attention, but it is not the present agenda.

What we have to do at the moment is to see that there are

varied insights and to remind ourselves that 'perhaps it is a law of nature that all children are different'.

Not long ago an English newspaper had the bright idea of taking some hundreds of photographs of women's faces at random and superimposing them all on top of each other. The result was interesting for what appeared on the final print was a face which conformed to all the standards—length of nose, position of eyes and so on—which, artists seem to suggest, constitutes the face of flawless beauty. Perfection was the distilled essence of a large number and each one of that number had made a contribution.

There is a direct relevance here to one of the deep strands of missionary motives. To put it in the words of Bishop Stephen Neill:

> Without yielding to any exaggerated idea of race or nation, it may yet be held that race, language and nation are a part of God's providential ordering of the world; and that, just as diversities of language and culture have been the means of drawing out to expression the varied riches and potentialities of the human spirit, so contact between the Gospel and varied national and cultural traditions is needed for the full explication of its treasures.[1]

The object of all English-based missions is not that Africans and Asians should become Englishmen. 'I am afraid that to some our message is no more than a foolish wish that the peoples of the world would please become middle-class Americans as soon as possible. This would be a solution to the world's aches. If 600 million Chinese would only go away and we could find 600 million middle-class Americans to take their places and sell electric typewriters to one another, this would be a mission easy to understand. But it is unlikely,' said Bishop Bayne to the General Convention at Detroit. And he thundered at his audience: 'God is not an American.'

The object of the mission of the Church is that everyone of

[1] *The Unfinished Task* (1957), p. 90.

every race should become what God intends him to become. Asians will not stop being Asians. They will be even more Asian as they become Asians-fulfilled-in-Christ. And Africans will become more African and Eskimos more Eskimo.

This, it appears, is one of those points where the divine purpose is being worked out in secular events. Canon Max Warren gives an interesting example:

> Will I be misunderstood if I say that what is emerging today is a distinctive African 'personality'? In saying that I do not at all pretend to underestimate the rich variety of life in Africa. But it is surely true that whereas even ten years ago what struck the traveller was the almost infinite diversity of Africa's peoples, today it is the increasing sense of their kinship which is making itself felt. It is this emergence of something which is African, and which, as African, is to be enjoyed, respected, understood and welcomed, which is so significant and so important, and so easily overlooked.[1]

The Church, of course, can claim little credit for fostering this 'Africanness'. But the Church should do all in its power to encourage—and sanctify—it. And not only for the sake of the African, but at the same time for its own enrichment.

The 1948 Lambeth Conference, indulging itself for a moment in more picturesque speech than was its wont, said it this way: 'The Anglican Communion today is like a river that is made up of streams, each of which passes through a different country, each with a colour drawn from the soil through which it passes, each giving its best to the full strength of the river, flowing toward that ocean symbolic of a larger comity when the Anglican Communion itself will once again become part of a reunited Christendom. No one stream is superior to another. The glory of each is its contribution to this river which, while being enriched by all, enriches all the countries of the world wheresoever it flows.'[2] If the Rhine were confined to Switzer-

[1]*CMS News-letter*, April 1962.
[2]*Report*, p. II. 83.

land it would be a very minor river and Germany would be much the poorer.

The whole world will have to go on fumbling in incompleteness until all are complete and each can share his gifts with all. Bishop Westcott realized that quite a time ago when he said that the final commentary on St John's Gospel would be written by an Indian. Only an Indian with a background of centuries of mystical probing on the banks of the Ganges or the Jumna is going to be equipped to pierce the mysticism of the great *Logos* doctrine and tell us bustling Westerners the depth of its meaning. Until then we can either hold ourselves in such patience as we can muster or we can seriously get on with the job of telling the Indian about Jesus Christ so that, knowing him, the Indian may lay his own peculiar gifts and national heritage, by then sanctified, at Christ's feet. And the same applies to the American Indian and to the Australian aboriginal and the rest of the races. God has shared his gifts among them all. And none shall be complete until all are complete. Like a father bequeathing to his sons a map which leads to buried treasure, God divides that map into one piece for each son, and none can reach the treasure until all pieces are fitted together.

All too often we imagine God wants us to have nothing but pure, unselfregarding motives, and none other, about his mission. God is a lot more merciful than that. He lets us get something out of it. He lets us learn the patience of the Chinese and the exuberance of the African and the activism of the American and all the rest of it. But we can learn these features and benefit from them fully only as we take to them the Christ in whom all men are fulfilled.

'John to the seven churches which are in Asia,' says the Bible. How very different they all were! Ephesus with its labour and patience and intolerance of evil, Smyrna with its works and tribulation and poverty, Pergamos with its faith, Thyatira which suffered Jezebel, Laodicea the lukewarm and so on. And when John had completed the roll call, 'I looked, and, behold, a door was opened in heaven.' The vision of God came when all the Churches, still retaining their different identities, were complete.

That is the vision we seek; but we are so anxious to anticipate its right moment. In a very real sense this chapter has been visionary in the most pejorative meaning of that word. We have been speaking largely of things as we would like them to be, and, even then, we have been limiting ourselves to the Anglican Communion. By our omissions we have laid ourselves open to the narcissism to which all Churches are heir. For the moment we are going to omit the ecumenical area of thought, though we recognize that without it any thinking is indeed bereft. For we must look at that word, narcissism. The dictionary says it means absorption in one's own perfections. The Anglican Communion, on that definition, has no ground for narcissism, for it has few, if any, perfections.

It is not even candid with itself about its own theory of national or regional Churches. Take Paris. There could be occasions when two Anglican bishops would be performing episcopal duties in the French capital on the same day at the same time and within a few hundred yards of each other. One would be American, one would be British. For Anglicans in Northern Europe have long been under the jurisdiction of the Bishop of London working through the Bishop of Fulham (it stems back to Archbishop Laud). On the other hand, the American theory of the wholeness of the Church and its solidarity causes them to maintain the pastoral care of American Anglicans in Europe. Something has gone badly wrong somewhere and so far no one has been able to put it right. It might be argued that there is nothing *theologically* wrong with this situation since neither the American nor the British bishop claims any territorial jurisdiction. They are both there to minister to chaplains and communities who are their own compatriots. Nevertheless, both American and British communities speak—more or less—the same language and it is hard to see any practical justification for what is surely a duplication of manpower.

But perhaps it can be argued that Christian Europe is not a natural field for Anglican work anyway, so the anomalies of a bit of overlapping work are not really important. In which case I draw your attention to Liberia. It is an American-based diocese in West Africa and its bishop has to return to America regularly to take his seat on such occasions as a General Convention. Meanwhile it is surrounded by the autonomous Anglican Province of West Africa with its own Archbishop and bishops, constitution and all the accoutrements of an ecclesiastical entity. So what we have in West Africa is an autonomous regional Anglican Church with a maverick Anglican diocese in its midst. This, of course, is not a problem of over-lapping jurisdiction specifically, but rather of provincial relationships. It comes, however, well within the area of our present concern.

A similar situation obtains in the Caribbean where you have an autonomous Anglican province—it has been independent since 1883—laced with American dioceses controlled from the United States. Two Churches for the organization of one, so to speak. Or is it two organizations for the one Church? No one who cares for God's Church can be happy about the schizophrenic way Anglicans operate in the Caribbean. Especially since the result is some sad anomalies. For example, people who can make their communion where they work but not where they live (since they live in one province and work in the other and the canons governing the status of people married after divorce differ quite sharply). Or again, in one part of the Caribbean the Anglican Communion bears one witness about family life and a quite different one in another, even though those parts are adjacent.

In fact, however, the confusion is not as bad as it might be, for the dioceses of the American Church are principally Spanish-speaking (or French, in Haiti) and are within the area of an inherited Spanish-Catholic tradition, while the Church of the West Indies is mainly an English-speaking body, concentrated in areas of a quite different racial and economic background.

Nevertheless, it will clearly be better and deeper for all concerned when the time comes for the establishment of a single
Caribbean Anglican Church.

Meanwhile, the Anglican falls back feverishly into his
history book and begins to explain the situation. The trouble
is that a nineteenth-century poultice has gone stale and will
not cure a twentieth-century boil.

The need to get all this sorted out presses hard for we are
busily engaged in producing a whole set of new problems.

For example, the 1948 Lambeth Conference had a resolution
(74) headed 'A Larger Episcopal Unity'. It reads: 'The Conference, welcoming the fact that some of the Churches of the
Anglican Communion are already in intercommunion with the
Old Catholic Churches, looking forward to the time when they
will enter into communion with other parts of the Catholic
Church not definable as Anglican, and desiring that Churches
thus linked together should express their common relationship
in common counsel and mutual aid, recommends that bishops
of the Anglican Communion and bishops of other Churches
which are, or may be, in communion with them should meet
together from time to time as an episcopal conference, advisory
in character, for brotherly counsel and encouragement.'

That is a long quotation but it is easily important enough
to be repeated in full. And Lambeth 1958 reaffirmed that resolution, and 'strongly recommends that within the next five years
the Archbishop of Canterbury should invite to a conference
representative bishops from each Province of the Anglican
Communion, together with representative bishops from each
Church possessing the historic episcopate with which churches
and Provinces of the Anglican Communion are in full communion or in a relation of intercommunion.'[1]

The relevance of all this to the idea of national or regional
Churches is obvious.

We have already commented on two Anglican bishops exer-

[1]*Report*, p. I. 35.

cising jurisdiction in Paris—and, of course, elsewhere in Europe. Now the Anglican Communion is in full communion with the Old Catholics—who have an archbishop and two bishops in Holland and bishops elsewhere in Europe. Can we imagine three bishops, one Old Catholic, one American Anglican, one British Anglican, all doing episcopal things in the same place at the same time, even if two of them claim they are ministering only to expatriate chaplaincies? And if, as could well be the case, any question of precedence arises, who begins to sort things out? Must one of the first and most urgent duties of a conference of 'a wider episcopal fellowship' be to appoint a Protocol Officer?

Is the suggestion absurd? So is the situation.

And Europe and the Old Catholics is not the only case in point. There is also the Spanish Reformed Episcopal Church (Iglesia Espanola Reformada Episcopal) in Spain, the Lusitanian Church (Igreja Lusitana Catolica-Apostolica-Evangelica) in Portugal, the Philippine Independent Church (Iglesia Catolica Filipine Independiente) in South-East Asia and the Polish National Catholic Church of America (an Old Catholic Church) in the United States. All these Churches are independent, reformed, Catholic Churches. They all have the historic succession. And they are all National Churches and could well express themselves in the Indian formula as being there to do for their countries what the Church of England has done in England.

It is perhaps in the Philippines and in the United States that the problem reaches its most acute form. In the Philippines you have two separate episcopates who are in full communion yet both claim the same territorial jurisdiction. One ministers mainly to Filipinos and one to the aboriginal peoples of the area. Similarly in the United States there are two separate episcopates—the Episcopal Church and the Polish Old Catholic Church—both in full communion and both exercising territorial and overlapping jurisdiction.

Both in the Philippines and in the United States it can be argued that each episcopate ministers to a different sociological and cultural group. Perhaps in a polyglot and pluralistic world the territorial episcopate must be left behind as a way of guiding, guarding and governing the Church. Perhaps there must be some study of the Roman pattern of the Uniat Churches or the Orthodox pattern of Exarchates. Perhaps indeed. But before we embark on it we must face the fact that we are abandoning what is involved in 'John to the seven churches which are in Asia . . .' The territorial episcopate is a concept rich in meaning and embedded deeply in the whole Anglican ethos. Modern circumstances are making it more difficult of realization than ever. But if we are going to be forced to relinquish it, we must at least struggle to retain everything it has of positive value— and that is much indeed. And we need to see our way very clearly to whatever complex organism (for this is a matter of *organism*, not organization) which must replace it.

Then again, what happens when these Churches become strong enough to sustain missions outside their own countries? Must we expect to see Anglican and non-Anglican bishops who are in full communion exercising separate but contiguous jurisdiction in churches across the road from each other in Delhi or Durban?

Old Catholics in Holland and Germany are already, praise be to God, operating outside their own countries. They have, however, found a *modus operandi* which seems to be adequate at least for the time being. Using the (Anglican) Society for the Propagation of the Gospel they have accepted invitations from Anglican bishops in Africa and elsewhere and are putting their resources into Anglican missions. Is this a viable pattern for all future extensions?

Perhaps at the rate at which *rapprochements* are developing, the question will find its own answer. The Bonn Agreement of 1931, for example, between Old Catholics and the Church of England, since taken up by other Anglican Provinces, established a pattern for such relationships. By its terms each recognizes the catholicity and independence of the other and maintains its own; each agrees to admit members of the other to participate in the sacraments; each believes the other to hold all essentials of the Christian Faith, but does not necessarily accept all doctrinal opinions, sacramental, devotional or liturgical practice characteristic of the other.

Some of these reformed Episcopal Churches, indeed, owe the historic succession of their episcopate to the Anglican Communion. As long ago as 1894, Irish Anglican bishops consecrated a Spanish Reformed bishop and Irish and American bishops consecrated his successor. The same happened in the cases of the Lusitanian Church and the Philippine Church. These Churches have Prayer Books essentially the same as Anglican Prayer Books and many other Anglican features. Yet they are not the result of Anglican missionary work. God has used neither the Church of England nor any of its sister Churches to bring them into being. Yet he has permitted to Anglican Churches the honour of befriending them and being a channel of their needs—such as the episcopate.

If these relationships do nothing else they ought to be able to convince Anglicans that they have no unique claim to anything that is Anglican. And if once we get that firmly in our minds and accept all its implications we shall probably see the way through all the problems of those hydra-headed monsters, nations with more than one national Church.

But we cannot leave the matter quite at that point. There are two more questions. How far should Anglicans encourage Anglicans to cease to be Anglicans and become members of a National Church which includes all that Anglicanism has to offer? The example of the Church of South India is one we still haven't worked out. North India, Lanka and others promise to follow in its train.

In two important articles in *Theology* (January and February, 1962), Dr Anthony Hanson points out that the more indigenous a church becomes, the more dependent it becomes on its fellow Christians of the same culture. He instances the 'continuing Anglicans' of Nandyal. Although the Metropolitan became their Ordinary, there were many things the Anglican

Church in North India could not do for them, for the Anglicans
of Nandyal speak Telugu, a language not used in the North.
So when they want textbooks or retreat conductors or whatever in their own tongue, it is to their non-Anglican cultural
group they must turn, rather than to their fellow-Anglicans
who are, culturally, foreigners.

'We are all agreed nowadays,' says Dr Hanson, 'that we want
the Church in Asia and Africa to become properly indigenous,
but we do not always recognize that the price to be paid for
this may be the strengthening of bonds with other local
Christians at the cost of the bonds with the world-denomination.
Indeed, it may well be that in some parts of the world the
Anglican character of our Church is purchased at the cost of
its indigenous character.'

Nor is this cultural compatibility the only factor. China
presents another type of lesson. The Chinese Anglican bishops
in this last decade have had no choice but to seek fellowship
with their non-Anglican fellow-Christians, who are Chinese,
rather than with their Anglican fellow-Christians, who are not
Chinese. Politics can be a very deterministic force at least in
the external life of the Church, and, in the sort of world we
live in, we cannot write China off as a forever unique example.
Communism and its curtains, in fact, do not really enter this
situation. It is easy to imagine circumstances in which *Africanness* would be much more important than *Anglican-ness* if
Christians had to stand together in the face of some non-
Christian Caesar somewhere within that continent.

We began our thinking about National Churches from a
Bible two thousand years old. We see that thinking having a
startling contemporary relevance as the world scene swims
before our eyes.

There is also another quite different question: as National
Churches grow in number, how are they going to demonstrate
that all God's people throughout the world are one family?
Earlier we had occasion to say that nationalism was a bad thing
only when it exists for the sake of its own nation alone. A

National Church which was like-minded would not be just a bad thing. It would be blasphemy. A National Church must, subject to the glory of God as always the first and over-riding consideration, exist for the sake of its own nation. But it must also exist for all mankind. How are those two facts to be reconciled?

I do not know the answer. Perhaps God feels we are not yet ready for an answer to be given. But I am convinced that it is high time we asked the question, and had it constantly on our minds and prayers.

For us who are Anglicans the question of the relationship of regional Churches is asked on at least two different levels. We have to ask it in regard to the relationship of the Anglican family to the greater Church beyond. The decade 1950-60 saw the creation of four new Provinces—as many as the previous half-century had produced. The next decade may produce as many or even more. Alongside these there is growing up a system of regional councils, the nature and function of which no one seems to understand very pellucidly. There is one in the American Caribbean, one in the Pacific and one in South East Asia. This last is the most highly developed and yet it seems to raise as many questions as it answers. Is it or is it not a synod? What degree of jurisdiction has it? To what degree does it have autonomy, for example, in dealing with non-Anglican Churches in its area? Perhaps it is considerations of geography and sociology which accentuate these questions. Perhaps the eventual aim is that the Council of South East Asia should grow into several provinces. Meanwhile it is an exciting development which galvanizes many questions.

And the great problem is how can these provinces, councils, maverick dioceses, and whatever, so act as to find common strength and yet respect individual integrity?

Such a question is important, yet it pales in comparison with that concerning the common action of all the Churches everywhere. And nothing less must be our goal—as it was our Lord's prayer. The days have gone when Christians could be satisfied

with some sort of 'invisible unity'. Today we must strive for
the existing unity of all in Christ to be translated into an
institutional reality. This applies not only in regard to the over-
coming of barriers of faith or order, but also to ensuring that
as regional Churches grow, no built-in geographical barriers
are allowed to grow with them. Each entity must preserve its
independence, but to independence must be added a sacramental
inter-dependence. Are we then envisaging one world Church
divided into units of National Churches, to each nation its
Church? The mind boggles at the thought, not least since
concepts of political sovereignty, despite all the nationalisms
of our day, seem to be weakening. Meditation on the European
Common Market might lead to the conclusion that the future
society, squeezed together by its own science, might be nearer to
the medieval than to the nation-states which have been the
general pattern of society in the last three hundred years.

We are, apparently, wandering from the meadows of Church
organization into the jungles of political alignments. Yet there
is inevitably a close relation between them. Quite obviously
one world Church would be a greater possibility if there were
one world State. There are those who suggest that in the world
of politics the United Nations Organization is a much closer
parallel to the Anglican Communion than is the British
Commonwealth.

But—and we recognize the fact with some sense of relief—
we are now trespassing beyond the bounds of this present book.
Our immediate concern is to look at that point where God has
placed us, in the Anglican Communion. And the Anglican
Communion has its own inescapable commitment to ask God
to tell it more of what is implied by 'John to the seven churches
which are in Asia . . .' The Anglican Communion is a federation of regional Churches, and must face all the perplexities
involved in that. As Bishop Bayne has said:

They are part of the travail of the Anglican household,
seeking to keep its generous heritage of national and regional

loyalties and at the same time find new means to fulfil its inner unity and meet the complex challenge of our world so terribly one and so profoundly inter-related. Nobody knows what the final answers will be, we are only at the beginning of all this, searching for a deeper unity in our diversity, seeking how to keep all the rich treasure of national and regional life and still act as one body, as the Church of Christ should act.[1]

[2]*Anglican World*, vol. i, no. I, p. 47.

3

Is Anglicanism a ' Confession '?

ONE OF the difficulties of Christian thinking is the facility that
words have for acquiring many meanings. It is even more a
difficulty of ecumenical discussion. And right in the middle of
ecumenical discussion today is this word 'Confession'. There
are not a few who suggest Confessionalism is a major, perhaps
the major, hindrance to the ecumenical movement. And Anglicans, especially in view of the Anglican Congress in Toronto
in 1963, are among those who are in the dock. For Toronto
1963 has been construed as a sort of annoyed Anglican
answer to the World Council of Churches and the whole
ecumenical movement. This is a very serious charge and we
must do something more than merely smile it off. If it is true
we must ask God to help us make it untrue. But if it is already
untrue, then maybe we have something to share with others,
even though they have not seen it yet.

Is the Anglican Communion a Confession or not? What is a
Confession anyway?

The *Oxford Dictionary of the Christian Church* presents a
variety of meaning in a brief compass. A 'confession' can be
the tomb of a confessor and can also mean an acknowledgement of sin. It can, in the sense St Augustine used it in his
famous title, mean an act of praise. And it can mean a profession of faith. It is this last sense and its derivatives that
concern us here. Quite clearly any confession of faith should be
a thing of which a man is proud, a thing he is prepared to stand
by. Yet nowadays it seems to have gained some pejorative

significance at least in some minds. 'Ah, so you are a Confession after all' sometimes has the smell of an accusation about it when the statement is made by a Protestant to an Anglican. There are even those who use the word to refer to a sort of ecclesiastical empire-building, the desire to set up an international power structure. The temptation to desire a unitary world denomination is present in many places. And it would be a world denomination which would over-ride the autonomy and responsibility of National Churches, thereby stifling their individuality and depriving the rest of the world of any peculiar gifts they might have to offer. This, clearly, is an evil and anyone is right to condemn it. It is also to take a perfectly good word and so distort its meaning that it becomes useless as a tool of human exchange. As far as this chapter is concerned Confessionalism means a corporate profession of faith which has been enunciated in at least a fair amount of detail on some given occasion.

The word 'Confession' as meaning a corporate statement of faith seems to have been first used about the ancient ecumenical creeds. But this connotation more properly begins its history in the sixteenth and seventeenth century and its father is Luther. On June 25th, 1530, at Augsburg, the Emperor Charles V was presented with a statement of belief which had been drawn up by Melanchthon and approved by Luther. The first half epitomizes Christian doctrine as defined by Luther and the second details abuses for which remedies were demanded.

In other words, it was a negative document. In the first place it specifically excluded all the things that Luther could not accept and in the second it protested *against* a situation. The fact that the situation was such that godly men could not accept it is true but, for the moment, is not our point. What we are concerned with is the fact that the positive desire to reform carries along with it the negative desire to protest, as well as the limiting desire to define. And it is this negative exclusiveness, shutting out those who do not view the Christian Faith from that particular point of view, which distinguishes the Confessional principle from the Church principle which has few closely defined exterior boundaries but is concerned to include as many as possible.

The Augsburg Confession was from the first an authoritative Lutheran manifesto and within a year the definitive edition was published. The shape of Lutheranism had been established and any Lutheran who wondered about some part of the Christian Faith henceforth had but to turn up the authority. Lutheranism had become a Confessional Church.

It is worth pausing for a moment to observe, in parenthesis, the most precise form in which the phrase 'Confessional Church' has been used. It is in connection with those German Evangelical Christians who, ranged around Martin Niemöller, most actively opposed the 'German Christian' Church Movement sponsored by the Nazis. The strength of a Confessional Church was amply demonstrated under Hitler by the martyr-like endurance of its members under persecution. And some of its positive fruits are obvious from the fact that these Christians were out primarily to profess their religious beliefs rather than to oppose political beliefs. They were *for* God rather than *against* Caesar and opposed Caesar only when their first loyalty forced it upon them.

There is no doubt that Anglicans have a great deal to learn from a body of Christians who can show they really stand for something. They remind us that the original word *protestare* has a very positive meaning of 'standing on behalf of'. And Anglicanism which, in the words of a cynic, is 'the Church which gives you a tiny inoculation of Christianity so that you are immunized against the real thing' could profit from that lesson.

We have used Lutheranism as an example of a Confessional Church. It is not the only one, of course. The current debate about Confessionalism would have little strength if it were. What is the area of this current debate? Like most Christian debates it refuses to be penned inside the fold and ranges round all the nearby mountains. But one focal point lies in the fact that at the very moment when the World Council of Churches is, for the first time in history, building up a world relationship of dissident Churches, most of these Churches are themselves engaged in building up world organizations which, superficially at least, must seem on many points to compete with, if not to conflict with, the World Council. Anglicans who go round confidently assuring others that Anglicanism is not a Confession may be reminded that Anglicanism sowed the seeds of this world organizational proclivity before anybody else did. No one could suggest that the first Lambeth Conference or several of its successors had the beginning of a suspicion that its activities could lead to any concept of a world organization. Yet the fact remains that the first Lambeth Conference was held in 1867 and it did call together bishops from most parts of the world. The Presbyterian World Alliance did not come into being until 1875, the Methodist Ecumenical Council until 1881, the International Congregational Union until 1891, the Baptist World Alliance until 1905 and the Lutheran World Federation until 1923 (what is the significance of the fact that the latest starter of that group has the most elaborate organization of all?).

What we have, then, is a series of world-wide families of Churches, most of which slightly antedate the historic events of the modern phase of the ecumenical movement and all of which appear to be stressing their own identity and vesting their own interests parallel with their relationship with the World Council of Churches.

We must remind ourselves that the World Council never has imagined and does not now begin to imagine itself as some super-Church, nor does it ever suggest that the deep differences of faith and order between the various Churches are frivolous and should be forgotten. Nevertheless, what we have is a situation in which the more the Churches get together, the more jealously each appears to be establishing its own identity and ensuring its own future. That the movement towards unity is simultaneously a movement towards self-identification of the various parts and clarification of why they are various is natural and proper. Yet the reasons why Confessionalism takes increasing time in the Christian debate must by now have become clear.

This is something we have to consider *as Anglicans*. What is the relevance of the Anglican Communion to Confessionalism? Is Anglicanism a Confession?

'Our ideal,' said the bishops at the 1930 Lambeth Conference, 'is nothing less than the Catholic Church in its entirety . . . We hold the Catholic faith in its entirety: that is to say, the truth of Christ, contained in Holy Scripture; stated in the Apostles' and Nicene Creeds; expressed in the Sacraments of the Gospel and the rites of the Primitive Church as set forth in the Book of Common Prayer with its various local adaptations; and safeguarded by the historic threefold Order of the Ministry.'[1]

Anglicans, in other words, believe in the Church as One, Holy, Catholic and Apostolic and can be content with nothing which circumscribes or diminishes this. Anglicanism, then, is not doctrinally a Confession.

Nor is it a Confession when we look at the matter historically. Anglicanism, as a statement of Christian faith and order, has no historical beginning. That remark must be carefully qualified. Christianity is a Faith based on historic events performed by God himself. Christianity begins with Christ and Christ is historical. But that is only partially true. For Christianity, in one sense, began before Christ. Otherwise the Old Testament would have no real relevance to Christ. Christianity began when God started preparing his world for the coming of the historic Christ. And that is far back among the indeterminate mists of prehistory. Anglicanism (which has, for example, a Prayer Book which looks back to both Temple and Synagogue) would claim that its roots went back into soil so deep that even the startling abilities of the modern historian accompanied by his brother the archaeologist cannot excavate

[1]*Report*, pp. 153-4.

them. All that the historian and the archaeologist do uncover supports the Christian theses. But they do not expose their *fons et origo*.

Anglicanism, then, has no historical beginning. But Lutheranism looks back to an actual day, June 25th, 1530.

And in the same way as Anglicanism cannot point to any actual date as its birthday, neither can it point to a founding father. There was a Mr Luther. There has never been a Mr Anglican. 'We call no man master,' said seventeenth-century divine, William Chillingworth. This, of course, may be due to an innate incapacity on the part of the English to take anything to its logical conclusion. Perhaps, indeed, the extremities of the sects were implicit in all that went to beget the Reformation. If so, the English failed to see this. It was the Greeks who first suggested that moderation shorn of all excess was a primary virtue. Were the English only too apt as students of the Athens of the fourth century B.C.?

Perhaps the Englishmen of the sixteenth century knew more about 'nothing in excess' than the Greeks themselves. However that may be, they never begot a dominating figure and so Anglicanism was never consciously worked out or deliberately determined by Henry VIII or Cranmer or anyone else. We must remind ourselves that Anglicans interpret the Reformation in terms of continuity not discontinuity. It is a process of continuity which, while it has numerous signal historical events, has no definable single historical origin. The continuity continues right back to the beginning. And, equally important, it also continues right up to the present.

Dr Molland has described it :

'The English Reformation was a moderate reform which adopted a conservative attitude towards the past. In matters of Church Order and Liturgy, it retained as much as possible of its Catholic heritage, and as a result England was less radical in its Reformation than countries with a Reformed (or Calvinist) or even a Lutheran tradition. The Church of England has persistently taken a conservative line coupled, however, with the will to institute reforms when these have been shown to be necessary.'[1]

When the Archbishop of Canterbury, Dr Ramsey, lectured at Athens University in May 1962 he had this conservatism in mind.[2] Speaking of the Caroline divines, he said:

> Their use of the Fathers led them particularly in two direc-
> tions. (1) They were led away from being preoccupied with
> the matters which had been the absorbing concern of the
> Continental Reformers, namely Justification and Predestina-
> tion, and became instead influenced by the proportion of the
> theology of the Fathers for whom the central doctrine was
> that of the Incarnation of the Word made flesh ... the In-
> carnation of the Son of God became the heart and centre of
> theology ... (2) The second trend in the Carolines, caused
> by their use of the Fathers, was this. Because they found in
> the Fathers the contrast of Greek and Latin theology they
> were saved from western narrowness, and were conscious that
> just as the ancient, undivided Church embraced both East
> and West so the contemporary Catholic Church was incom-
> plete without the little-known Orthodox Church of the East
> as well as the familiar Churches of the West—Latin, Re-
> formed and Anglican. Hence there begins, in the heart of
> the Anglican theology, a yearning towards the East ... In
> both these ways the use of the ancient Fathers helped the
> divines of our English Church to realize in depth, width,
> and balance the meaning of the appeal to Scripture and
> Antiquity which our reformers had made. The meaning was
> this: not only that the Church of England looked back to
> the undivided Church as a guide or pattern, but that the
> Church of England claimed to be one with the undivided
> Church in actual continuity.

The story of the Church of England and Anglicanism is a story of continuity. Anglicanism, in other words, is not a Faith which has finally arrived, but a Faith which is always in process of becoming.

[1]*Christendom*, p. 141.   [2]*Canterbury and Constantinople* (1962), pp. 4-5.

To quote Dr Langmead Casserley.[1]

> As Anglicans read their own history, and understand and interpret all Christian history through their own historical experience, the Reformation stands out as a genuine *refor-mation* of a pre-existing reality which was provided for and given to Anglicanism by its pre-Anglican history. It is an episode in Anglican existence and not the beginning of Anglican existence. When Anglicans go back to the beginnings they return, like the great reformers themselves, not to the reformers but to the patristic Christianity of the early Church and ultimately to the Apostolic witness itself. The lack of any semi-idolatry of the reformers is something which Anglicans have in common with the reformers. Conversely, the exaggerated deference to the opinion of the reformers characteristic of so many of the Reformation churches is something which sharply distinguishes these churches from the reformers.

A little later in his argument Dr Casserley continues:

> The essence of Anglicanism is to be expressed in terms of what it is now visibly becoming, and will more and more become . . . whereas the essence of Protestantism is to be found in the original protest of the great reformers rather than in what Protestantism has since become and is more and more becoming. Protestantism is a great historical *event*; Anglicanism is a great historical *process*. They demand different categories of interpretation because they differ in nature . . . The grandeur of Anglicanism is not to be found in the original Anglican *via media*; though from the first pregnant with promise of what was to come, it is in every way inferior to the Anglican synthesis which we can now see to be emerging. On the other hand the original protestantism of the reformers is infinitely superior to contemporary protestant systems. Protestantism is at its best when it takes the form of a 'back to the reformers' movement; Anglicanism is at its best when it takes the form of an 'onwards to the Anglican synthesis' movement.

[1] *Christian Community* (1960), p. 112.

The Anglican Communion is not an end in itself. It is a part of our present, given situation. Its destiny is to disappear into something which, being greater than itself, includes all the insights Anglicanism has. Anglicanism has its gifts. But they are gifts which must be shared, given away, before they can be fully enjoyed.

We have to keep those gifts in good condition until we can hand them over. Nothing shop-soiled, second-hand or unkempt is going to be good enough for this coming Great Church. But we are going to fail in our duty if we keep our eyes so firmly fixed on our gifts that we get mesmerized into an orgy of soul-rotting self-admiration. In any case, we are not going to be able to assess the value of our gifts properly unless we also look at the other person's. At which point the devil and quite a cohort of his angels are waiting to pounce. There is a perennial temptation to that most sinful and intellectually dishonest form of ecumenical uncharity; are we trying to compare other people at their worst with ourselves at our best? Are we comparing what other people do with what we merely claim to do?

We have no right to compare anyone with anyone. That is getting too near an act of judgement and we are firmly assured that 'there is one that judgeth' and judgement must be left to him. But equally he has directed us to seek him who is all truth. And the search for truth does involve looking at all the possibilities and taking a personal decision about them. We are concerned all the time not to write an *apologia* for Anglicanism. If it is true, it doesn't need such, and if it is not true, none of our words will make it so. Our constant concern must be to see how God wants us to go about the Father's business and be in Christ who is reconciling the world unto himself.

The moment we say that we are forced to realize once more that what we are really concerned with is action rather than thinking. It may not be activism in the modern sense of the word. It may be just waiting upon God. But we are called to action. That does not deprecate the theologians and the philosophers nor does it suggest that it doesn't matter what you believe as long as you act like an English gentleman. But it does assert that cerebration is not an end in itself.

To quote Dr Molland again:[1]

> The Anglican Communion, unlike the Lutheran, assigns a primary place to questions of Church Order. In the Anglican view it is just as vital for the Church to have a right order as it is to have the right doctrine. This attitude becomes apparent in the ecumenical discussions of the present day in which Anglicans strongly advocate certain principles of Church Order. The watchword 'Faith and Order' is a typically Anglican formulation.

Which brings us back to an accusation then made against Anglicans. 'They have no theology,' says the critic. 'They are forever disagreeing with each other about so many points.' (This is not the same as the accusation that Anglicans have no specifically *Anglican* theology, a point with which we deal elsewhere: it is a charge that we have no theology at all.)

The accusation is interesting because it is both true and false. To quote Dr Wand:[2]

> It is sometimes said, even by its friends, that the trouble with Anglicanism is that it has no theology. That surely must be wrong. Did Hooker and Jewell, Pearson and Bicknell live in vain? If it is meant that we have no comprehensive and articulated system like the *Institutes* of Calvin or even the *Decrees* of the Council of Trent, it is true enough. But it is already something of a theology to deny the necessity for binding such burdens, grievous to be borne, on men's shoulders. If it is meant that we have no special and peculiar doctrines of our own, that too may be taken as part of our glory. We claim to believe what is in the creeds and in the Bible, that is to say, what is common to all Christendom. We

[1]*Christendom*, p. 165.
[2]*Anglicanism in History and Today*, p. 227.

have our Catechism and our Articles, although we regard them as on a lower level of authority than the creed. The Lambeth Conference of 1888 declared that missionary churches 'should not necessarily be bound to accept in their entirety the Thirty-nine Articles of Religion'. It is probably just this refusal to be wise above what is written or to regard every doctrinal issue as closed that makes the critics regard Anglicans as lacking a theology.

That reference to the Thirty-nine Articles does bring into focus the point at which the Church of England was nearest to becoming a Confessional Church. The Articles might even be described as an attempt to show how far an Anglican can go in the direction of becoming Confessional without becoming Confessional. At every point Anglicanism draws back from the final step. It goes in the direction of Lutheranism—but only just so far. And in the direction of Calvinism—but soon calls a halt. The Thirty-nine Articles are not a credal statement nor the exposition of a creed. They are rather short summaries of Christian belief and opinion which avoid any careful and precise definition. And their essence lies in the fact that they were an attempt to set out the Church of England's dogmatic position not in any eternal context but in strict relation to the controversies of their day. Their day is nearly four centuries ago and today is a new day. The controversies have largely disappeared, so they can now be variously interpreted without imposing undue strain on logic or credibility. And in any case, as we have said, these Articles are a Church of England document and are not part of the general pattern of the Anglican Communion.

They are not a representative sample of the literature produced by Anglican divines. Anglicans, as it happens, do have a noble tradition of theological writing. Not for nothing has their learning sometimes been awarded the title *stupor mundi*. Anglicans have written theology and non-Anglicans have found it worth their time to look at it. But there are two points. A great number of the leading Anglican theologians over the years have not been men who have been full-time theologians. They have always had other duties—Dr Michael Ramsey is a notable contemporary example of what we mean. Few would deny him status as a theologian yet none would deny that being Bishop of Durham, Archbishop of York and Archbishop of Canterbury, his successive offices, are reasonably full-time jobs. Even when Anglicans scale theological heights they frequently do so as a secondary occupation. The second point stems from the first. Great Anglican theologians have rarely been theologians for the sake of theology. Somehow their theology has avoided becoming an academic abstraction. It has certainly not been an activity which could be relegated to some watertight compartment. That would be impossible for those who are fellow-members with, say, Hooker, whose sweep so included both reason and revelation that everything got caught up into it. 'Anglicans,' says Bishop Wand, 'have always found it difficult to separate sharply between the sacred and the pro-fane.' Anglicans, indeed, have been accused of being worldly, and no doubt the accusers would give the word a most unwelcome connotation. But it was William Temple who described Christianity as the most material of all religions.[1]

Dr Ramsey has noted how modern Anglican divines make the Incarnation the centre of their teachings:

> But more specially they used the doctrine of the Logos to show that all that is good and true in philosophy, in science, in civilization, is caused by the divine Logos who is at work in all the world as the light that lighteth every man. In the last century the Church in the West was embroiled in the problems caused by modern scientific study. There was the theory of Evolution taught by biologists. There was the rise of historical criticism, with its corollary in the criticism of the Holy Scriptures. There was the rise of new forms of scientific culture. In the midst of this scientific revolution the Church had an anxious task, and I think that this conflict was felt more acutely in the West than in the East. What

[1]*Canterbury and Constantinople*, p. 7.

was the Church to do? It was possible to try to defend the faith as inside an ark, and to regard all science and philosophy outside the Church as an enemy. That was the method of Tertullian. But it was also possible to invoke the doctrine of the Logos as taught most notably by St Irenaeus, and the attitude and temper seen most notably in St Clement of Alexandria. That was the method followed by some notable Anglican theologians, such as Bishop Charles Gore, in facing the new discoveries of science. Using the doctrine of the Logos, they were able to show that modern scientific studies are no enemy but have within them the working of the divine Logos who is ever in the world.

Anglicans have been described as 'worldly'. But is it not true to describe the God who loved the world so much that he gave his own son as being 'worldly'. Anglicans are not prepared to yield one jot of this world to any other domination than God's. It is not a region in which he feels a bit out of place or a realm where he is lost. He reigns and it is his kingdom, even though he has let men and evil pollute it. Anglicans have noted that and have, accordingly, let themselves get wrapped up in the world not only as the arena of God's acts of salvation but as itself one of the objects of that salvation. The result has been that their theology must always be in the given situation. And, being a comprehensive theology, its edges become indeterminate as it reaches out into the world—as it becomes incarnate in the world.

It is not true to say that Anglicans do not know any theology. Rather the truth is that they have always seen theology as a means rather than an end in itself.

A means to what? To living under obedience to God, who is infinite, and therefore comprehends every extreme. Perhaps the secret of Anglicanism lies just there. For it has been termed a dialectic faith, one which deliberately accepts the tension between different points of view.

Dr Langmead Casserley has something important to say about this:[1]

[1] *Christian Community*, p. 111.

We may describe the movement of Anglican history as one from compromise to synthesis, from the middle way to the total way. It begins by steering cautiously between two extremes but we can already see, in the light of more than four centuries of history, that it can only end by comprehending the two extremes, by including two points of view which, through a series of lamentable historical accidents, have come to interpret themselves as antithetical, in one rich, coherent synthesis which will enable us to recover the wholeness of the Catholic Faith.

Dr Casserley is a long way from Simon Patrick, a seventeenth-century Anglican Divine who contested 'the virtuous mediocrity' of his own Church with 'the meretricious gaudiness' of the Church of Rome and 'the squalid sluttery of the fanatic conventicles.' Simon Patrick, of course, could support his *via media* from the 1662 Prayer Book Preface: 'It hath been the wisdom of the Church of *England*, ever since the first compiling of her Publick Liturgy, to keep the mean between the two extremes, of too much stiffness in refusing, and of too much easiness in admitting any variation from it.'

What are we to say about the apparent contrast between the seventeenth-century yearning for the Middle Way and today's desire to comprehend the two extremes? The phrase *via media* occurs too frequently in a pejorative context for anyone to imagine that twentieth-century Anglicans regard 'a virtuous mediocrity' as the final aim. In the first place, the longing for a *via media* was born out of a given historical situation where the extremes of the Church of Rome and the extremes of Protestantism both appeared in their worst light. The Liturgical Movement has shed a new beam on both. In the second place, the contrast between longing for a *via media* and a desire for a comprehension of both poles and the annihilation of neither is not as real as it appears. In the third place, the whole process of the shift of emphasis from one to another is itself a mark of the vocation of Anglicanism to be a Faith which is in process of becoming, not a Faith which has ossified into finality.

'What we have to look for in the ecclesiastical literature of England is not so much finality as direction; and if this implies a degree of inconsistency among those groping for the way, such pliancy of mind in approaching the mysteries of revelation may prove safer than premature fixation.'[1] Anglicanism certainly need make no apology for the fact that it is thus incomplete. Change and growth are basic conditions of this life. The acorn that remained an acorn could never be a church pew or reredos—nor give birth to other acorns.

We must return to Dr Casserley's idea (though he is not unique in holding it) of the movement from the Middle Way to the Total Way. How far is he weaving the gossamer threads of a philosopher's study in such a dream? The state of the Church of England today as compared with any period in the last four hundred years provides an illuminating example. The great Evangelical Revival of the late eighteenth century was followed by the Oxford Movement in the nineteenth. Each had its own particular insight and by the time those apparently antithetical insights had been brought into tension the sparks were flying. The latter part of the nineteenth century extending over into the twentieth were days when some of the most celebrated cases in the civil courts were on ecclesiastical offences. The Church of England had degenerated in some ways to a series of dogfights.

The mid-twentieth century picture is very different. The Church is at peace with itself and is, surely, more healthy and more alive than it has been for many generations. Yet neither the Evangelical nor the Oxford Movement insight has been lost and the synthesis so far achieved, which can be only a bit of the total still to be achieved, is something rich and fertile.

Behind this Anglican attitude there is a very profound and basic theology—in the truest sense of that word, because it is concerned with God. The sort of God we believe in is not only one who made the world at the beginning. He also keeps it going. He not only created us when we were born. He is still

[1]*Anglicanism*, ed. P. E. More and F. L. Cross, p. xx.

in the process of making us. He not only created his Church. He is still engaged in making his Church and the final form of that Church remains known only to him. As long as Anglicans can let the initiative remain with God they need not worry because they are in a process of becoming.

Anglicans are not a body of people bound together by common thought which can be expressed in terms of common doctrinal statements covering every aspect of faith and order. Their common thought is the sort which leads to common action—and especially the common action of the Breaking of the Bread which they share with their Lord and each other.

Bishop Bayne has given us a memorable quotation on this subject. He was speaking of the Eucharist which was part of the Inauguration ceremony for the Province of Uganda and Ruanda-Urundi:

> For here were these hundreds of Africans, with their hands outstretched to receive the Bread. I could not communicate with them, for the language barrier lay between us. My life, my culture, my background were totally different from theirs. I was only too keenly aware of my limitations as a provincial Westerner, separated from them by a thousand factors over which I had little control. Yet the unity of the Church was perfectly clear; and it was a unity established not by words or constitutions or formulas, but by Bread. This was the basis of the unity. As their hands reached forward to hold the Bread, so did mine; and somehow our differences began to disappear, in the enormous and wonderful and somehow frightening unity of the Bread. I don't know whether this remembrance can communicate to anybody else what it does to me. But I know that I shall never forget the way in which I was recalled to a true sense of the unity of Christ's Body—the way in which the Church remembered its real nature—in that simple act.[1]

There is something here which goes beyond the threshold of words, and it is vital. We call it Full Communion and we wonder

[1]*Mindful of the Love*, p. 21.

what we mean even as we say the words. It is the high point of all human relationships under God. It is the fulfilment of all that happened in Baptism. It is something so different from the 'hospitality' that two Churches still in disunion can extend to each other: in such cases either the appreciation of the Holy Mysteries is inadequate or there is something unreal, almost illicit, in accepting them across the chasm of schism. When Anglican Churches receive the Sacrament at each other's altars they are not just coming together in a symbolic act. There is something much deeper, more meaningful than that. This does not mean that all Anglicans think alike in regard to the Eucharist, but it does mean that all are involved in each other in a host of ways which are crystallized in the sacramental involvement. When Bishop Bayne, an American, shared with Africans in that Uganda Eucharist, he knew—it was part of the climate of his thought, part of the warp and woof of his experience—that he was sharing with fellow-Anglicans who were what they were because Anglican missionaries had gone to them, Anglicans had prayed and sacrificed for them, Anglicans had become one with them. There was no need to recite any Confessional formula—the Nicene Creed cannot be called such. There was no need for anything except acceptance. This could be no mere act of hospitality for you cannot be hospitable to your own family. You can only accept them ineluctably as your brothers with precisely the same right as yourself to your patrimony. The right to the patrimony, of course, springs not primarily from the brotherhood but from the Fatherhood. Being brothers, of itself, guarantees no inheritance. Only if the Father has provided it does it become yours. The objective reality of the Sacrament is dependent on the Father, and its recognition as such is the grounds of its meaningfulness. This book dare not presume to develop into a treatise on Eucharistic theology. Yet here lies the heart of the agenda for Anglicans and we must record it. We can do no more. We dare do no less.

Anglicans act together in regard to the Sacrament, but it does not mean they act together in all things. Some, for example, are pacifists and some are not, some vote Conservative or Republican and some don't vote at all. Anglicans don't come in one pattern, in all details, off one production belt, but they do all accept the same baptism, the same ministry, the same Bible, and the same common Table. They also, of course, share so much else—a common treasury of ideas, a common idea of freedom and responsibility, a common history—but they do not attempt to formulate such things in a definable constitutional statement. It is such a constitutional statement which both defines a Confession, gives it its unity, and, at the same time, divides and differentiates it from other Churches.

Anglicans share many things and these knit them together. But they also insist on preserving many things which would appear to be causes of fragmentation and fission, potentially if not in realized fact. 'We, Archbishops and Bishops of the Holy Catholic and Apostolic Church in communion with the See of Canterbury, three hundred and ten in number, assembled from forty-six countries ...' are the opening words of the Encyclical Letter of the last Lambeth Conference. They do not mention the Anglican Communion. Nor do they suggest any closer relationship with each other than 'in communion with'. You must have more than one entity if there is to be communion. You cannot share with yourself. The Anglican Communion is not a world Church but a world fellowship of Churches. The classical statement on this point was at Lambeth 1930:

> This (Anglican) Communion is a commonwealth of Churches without a central constitution: it is a federation without a federal government. It has come into existence without any deliberate policy.... They (the Churches) are, in the idiom of our fathers, 'particular or national' Churches, and they repudiate any idea of a central authority other than Councils of Bishops.[1]

Lambeth 1930 went on to foresee the 'commonwealth of Churches' becoming quite as odd an agglomeration as the

[1]*Lambeth Conference*, 1930, *Report*, pp. 28, 29.

British Commonwealth of Nations has become by the early sixties. 'Every Church of our Communion is endeavouring to do for the country where it exists the service which the Church of England has done for England ... As the Churches more and more fully achieve this purpose, they may, in many ways, grow less and less like to each other and to their Mother, and, in consequence, less and less Anglican, though no less true to Catholic faith and order.' This, as the bishops said, was to 'anticipate (a) progressive diversity'. All of which are not the words of a body which has any sense of being or any ambitions towards becoming a Confessional Church.

The Anglican Communion expects a diversification. Yet every Anglican Christian anywhere in the world is automatically a member of the Anglican Communion anywhere in the world. That is not paralleled in the Lutheran World Federation. Undoubtedly the most highly developed Confessional organization in the world, not all Lutheran Churches are members of it. Nor are all Lutheran Churches members of the World Council of Churches. Anglicanism, which apparently has so little to hold it together, manages to act in concert. Lutheranism, so much more integrated, so much more defined, shows within itself the fissiparity so characteristic of the Reformation. Does this suggest that unwritten constitutions are more durable than those which are written? A written constitution is of necessity the product of a certain age and a certain group and has their defects as well as their virtues. An unwritten constitution is usually something which has been built up by trial and error over the centuries. It therefore does not bear the marks of a given historical situation which may be irrelevant today.

The Church of England bears curiously few marks of the historical situation at the time of the Reformation. Many that are held to be such disappear on inspection. For example, some believe that the power of the Crown in the appointment of bishops was an invention of Henry VIII. Long before Henry was thought of William the Conqueror had a very large hand in such appointments and he showed his temper very clearly when the Pope tried to curtail his powers. Again, the fact of Establishment did not begin when a fawning and subservient Church sold itself to some monarch. It has developed imperceptibly throughout English history. Indeed, the Church of England was an entity before the kingdom of England was, so that a relationship was inevitable when the kingdom came into being.

The Anglican Communion, quite certainly, shows few marks of being the product of any given historical situation. Those who suggest it came into existence merely as the British Empire's Religious Division need to read more history. They also must remember that in places like Japan, Korea, the Philippines, South America, Madagascar, and elsewhere, the British Empire never had any influence, but the Anglican Communion is there.

Perhaps if the Anglican Communion had more of the historian's brandmarks upon it, it would be easier to talk about it. But it has not. And, accordingly, we say that it lacks the homogeneity and, in a limited sense of the word, integrity to become a Confession. It also lacks that other characteristic of a Confession, the fact that by very virtue of its definition it excludes others. Now let us be clear about this. The Anglican Communion is not a broad gate opening on to a nebulous path which beckons all, irrespective of faith or order. To many its insistence on proper episcopal order, for example, constitutes a very high barrier and is the mark of an uncompromisingly exclusive Church. Yet no one can deny that the path of twentieth-century ecumenicity is lit by many Anglican lights. Brent, Azariah, Bell, Temple, Fisher ... the names are legion. The Anglican yearning against exclusiveness is an ever present pain at its heart. It seems to lead Anglicans, more than most, to disregard their own rules and to indulge in acts of open Communion. This does not mean that non-Anglicans do not take part in open Communions. It is just that they break fewer of their Church's rules when they do so. The very ability of an Anglican to break his Church's rules is a demonstration that this Anglican Communion lacks the clear definition of a Confession.

Anglicans have a yearning towards Church unity which has flowered in many acts. Primary among them must be the famous *Appeal to All Christian People* made by the bishops at Lambeth in 1920. That Appeal is surely significant enough in itself. It becomes still more charged with meaning when it is seen in context.

In the first place, of the eighty resolutions passed by the 1920 Lambeth Conference no less than twenty-two—over a quarter —were concerned with unity.

Of deeper significance still is the fact that that Appeal came from a Conference which included Bishop Hensley Henson and Bishop Frank Weston, representatives of very different views. Both had gone to the Conference with strong emotions and they seemed little disposed to make concessions. Weston had been the source of an indictment against his neighbouring bishops of Uganda and Mombasa, an indictment which threatened to split the Anglican Communion. The first World War had submerged the 'Kikuyu controversy', as the result of Weston's indictment was called, but it had not brought any solution. The Lambeth Conference of 1920 met with two highly charged poles ready to produce the searing spark which would char the lot. And it ended in reconciliation and an *Appeal to All Christian People*. The Anglican Communion had found its own unity the hard way and had found, too, what a treasure it was. And so it went straight out to share it with others.

Now the circumstances of the 1920 Conference were not the circumstances of a Confession. And even more, the *Appeal* was not the sort of document which a Confession would normally be expected to originate. It is the work of a Church which yearns for comprehension.

Having said that the visible unity of the Church will involve a ministry acknowledged by every part of the Church as possessing not only the inward call of the Spirit but also the commission of Christ and the authority of the whole body, the bishops continue: 'May we not reasonably claim that the Episcopate is the one means of providing such a ministry? It is not that we call in question for a moment the spiritual reality of the ministries of those Communions which do not possess the Episcopate. On the contrary we thankfully acknowledge that these ministries have been manifestly blessed and owned by the Holy Spirit as effective means of grace.'[1]

They even went on further to say: 'If the authorities of other Communions should so desire, we are persuaded that, terms of union having been otherwise satisfactorily adjusted, Bishops and clergy of our Communion would willingly accept from these authorities a form of commission or recognition which would commend our ministry to their congregations, as having its place in the one family life.'

The hope was that the non-episcopally ordained would be led by the same motive to seek episcopal ordination.

Lest anyone should still misunderstand, the bishops also added: 'In so acting no one of us could possibly be taken to repudiate his past ministry. God forbid that any man should repudiate a past experience rich in spiritual blessings for himself and others . . .'

Those words had wide publicity and without any question had a real effect on the people of their day. Have they had any effect since? The answer cannot but be in the affirmative; but to assess that effect is both beyond the competence of the present writer and also outside our present scope.

What we are concerned to deduce from them in addition to their ecumenical lesson is the insight into the Anglican mind that they provide.

It is a mind which at all times seems as much aware of what we do not know as of what we do know. A mind which keeps on reminding itself that what we are dealing with in all these things is God himself and all his relationships with men and therefore their relationships with each other. We are dealing

[1]*Lambeth Conferences*, 1867-1930, p. 39.

with God and if we try to squeeze him into our narrow measurements and definitions we lose him in the process. It is a mind which always allows for the possibility of human error. For that reason a true Anglican cannot be partisan in the sense that he is wholly right and the others are wholly wrong. It is a state of mind which requires humility, and Anglicans have no more natural propensity to that virtue than any others. But the ethos in which their minds and souls have been nurtured has helped them at least to see where that virtue lies. The rigour of a Confessional statement with its resulting comfort and conviction is denied to them. All they can be certain about is the evidence of the Bible interpreted by the Church and crystallized by the Creeds. To formulate in greater detail must remain a luxury to which they cannot attain.

Perhaps Anglicans cannot help remembering that in the very first book of the Bible the one thing which was denied to Adam was the tree of final knowledge, the knowledge which is so complete that it imprisons the mind and leaves no room for any act of faith. They admit they cannot even bind the sweet influence of the Pleiades or loose the bands of Orion or guide Arcturus with his sons. How then can they reduce God to some final, definitive formula? But equally, since to know God is the true end of man, how can they desist from the adventure of tracing his paths? So they live in tension, searching a pilgrim's way, seeking the city. And their guiding flare is their sense of continuity with the Great Church which has marched down the ages and throughout the world.

If they can do it with the sanctity of Bishop Thomas Ken (died 1711), God will surely bless their efforts. In his will he wrote: 'I die in the Holy Catholic and Apostolic faith, professed by the whole Church before the division of East and West; more particularly I die in the Communion of the Church of England, as it stands distinguished from all papal and puritan innovations.'[1]

---

[1]There is a valuable discussion by David M. Paton in his book *Anglicans and Unity* (1962).

4

The Administration of Mission: in Principle

ADMINISTRATION IS a word which has attracted many caustic comments. In most areas of life today size has become a seemingly inescapable element; and administration seems to accompany size like income tax accompanies government. Administration, its philosophy and its science, has produced a great volume of literature and its prophet, Professor Parkinson, has added many new phrases to our vocabulary.

The dictionary suggests that administration means management and one can easily see why men therefore fear it. 'O God, don't let the machinery get me' is the reported prayer of a Canadian Church leader and he no doubt spoke for many. Yet is this not one more case of the best being corrupted to become the worst? Right at the heart of the word is another—minister. The Christian must accordingly search for the relation between administration and the Christ who said, 'I am among you as he who ministers.' If Christian administration is indeed the considered putting into practice of the injunction of the Servant to be among men as those who serve, then it clearly deserves the time a Christian can give to studying it.

That is an eminently theological reason for considering it. There is also an eminently practical reason.

We believe the Church is the household of the Spirit who blows where he lists. No man can tell where the next evidence of his operation will manifest itself. Yet that Spirit knows we are human, and human beings must work through human channels. A Church which buries its talent in the ground of pietism or wishful thinking will escape censure no less than the man in the Gospels who wasted his opportunities. The whole of the corporate Christian life of the Church consists in providing the channel through which the things of heaven find expression among the things of earth and vice versa. Whether it is a matter of making as perfect as possible a purely Godward act of worship or making as manifest as possible a purely manward act of God, administration is called for. 'Let all things be done decently and in order', said St Paul, and he thereby became the apostle of administration. This does not mean Paul was unspiritual. It is just that the spiritual was so important that it called for the best in its physical presentation and hallows that physical presentation in the process.

While this chapter is concerned with the administration of the Church's Mission, we cannot but let ourselves be momentarily diverted to be reminded of what that mission is about— if only to try to escape the fate of those who let the means obscure the end. In any case, those who spend much time talking about the Church's Mission will be only too devastatingly aware of the infinite number of wrong ideas there are about what the Mission really is.

The basic statement of the Christian Faith is that God loved the world so much that he sent his son into it. God sent Christ. But the word 'sent' is the same as the word 'mission'. God loved the world so much that his Son became a missionary. But Christ is supreme in everything, so he cannot be *a* missionary, one among many. He must be *the* Missionary, *par excellence*. But you can distinguish between a missionary and his mission. There is, however, no distinction in Christ. So we reach the statement: God loved the world so much that Christ became his Mission.

Now, we repeat, Christ is supreme in everything. So that must mean that Christ is God's *total* Mission to the world. How, then, is there any mission left for us? Humanly speaking there is not. Humanly speaking we just do not have any mission. Christ is all in all.

But Christ said, 'I am the vine, ye are the branches.' And he said that any servant of his would be so empowered that 'The works that I do shall he do also; and greater works than these shall he do.'

By our baptism we are made members, parts, of Christ and the part, however inadequately, has the nature of the whole. So, then, by our baptisms we too become totally Mission in Christ. It is not that we *have* a mission. We *are* mission because we are in Christ. The Lambeth Conference of 1958, echoing an earlier conference at Willingen in 1952, said the same thing in more impressive words, 'There is no participation in Christ without participation in his mission to the world.'

We then *are* mission, total mission to the whole world and our lives remain unfulfilled if we fail to recognize and act upon that fact. And as each baptized Christian is mission, so the whole Church, *a fortiori*, is mission.

So far the argument is unassailable. Mission is the nature of the Christian Church. But how to fulfil that mission? What sort of management, organization, administration? It is perhaps a further demonstration of the comprehensiveness of the Anglican Communion that such questions can be asked and lively arguments arise over the answers. Other Churches have a single system. Anglicans have an exuberant chaos. Other Communions can say firmly, 'This is the way we do Mission.' Anglicans can only respond, 'We are trying every method that human ingenuity, with or without the assistance of the Holy Spirit, could ever think up.'

Now one thing must be firmly asserted. Anglicans know perfectly well that the Church is Mission and that Mission and Church are inseparable. (That sentence, the intelligent reader will not need to be told, calls for qualifications. Not *every* Anglican 'knows perfectly well'. A long way from it! But Anglicanism knows perfectly well that Church and Mission are one. You cannot have one without the other.)

But, says the reader, what about all those societies they have in England? How can they be justified as against the unitary system whereby the fact that the Church and Mission are one is patent and whereby the administration of the Mission is done by an official department of the Church in its central organization?

Those are questions, I believe, which God is asking us to ponder deeply. In any case they cannot be sidestepped in a book like this.

There are some preliminary statements to be made. First is a declaration of what might appear (though I sincerely trust that such appearance is deceptive) to be a vested interest. For eleven years and more it has been my absorbing privilege to work for the Society for the Propagation of the Gospel, England's oldest missionary-sending society (founded 1701).[1] Yet I believe I can honestly say that I am not really interested in S.P.G. for the sake of S.P.G. S.P.G. has my loyalty because it is, in itself, quite insignificant. Like the other societies of the Church of England, S.P.G. constantly reminds itself that it is a handmaid, a tool. It repeats to itself constantly that Mission is the work of the Church. S.P.G. just happens to be a particularly experienced instrument. Perhaps such an apologia will at least diminish the more unfortunate implications of any vested interest when we are trying to think clearly of all the pros and cons of the unitary and society systems of fulfilling the one Mission. And will also silence the critic who suggests I am claiming for S.P.G. some virtue unique among the English societies.

The second preliminary statement is this: the Anglican Communion is particularly Anglican in its administration of Mission because nowhere in the world, it seems, can either the unitary or the society system be found in a pure form.

To take the unitary system first. The United States and Canada spring to mind as the first examples. Both the Overseas Department of the National Council and the Missionary Society of the Anglican Church in Canada are official depart-

---

[1] S.P.C.K., founded three years earlier, specializes more in the printed word than in the sending of living agents.

ments answerable to the central authorities of their churches. As such, that is the unitary system. But in the United States you have lively youngsters like the Overseas Mission Society, and the Episcopal Churchmen for South Africa organization, while in Canada you have the Women's Auxiliary. Few would deny that those bodies are making real contributions to the overseas Mission of their Churches. Bishop Bayne has stated his opinion of the Overseas Mission Society:

> The vocation of the Overseas Mission Society is to be a path-finder for the Church, able to take risks, to experiment, to improvise, to agitate, to excite, to fail, to succeed and then pass over to the Church the results of success ... Ought not the Overseas Mission Society to pioneer a project (perhaps in connection with Brazil?) which would help us all in studying and understanding the growth-needs of new dioceses, the criteria for provincial status, the whole process of growing up?[1]

Furthermore, there is a significant reaching out from the ordinary churchgoers in North America to the missionary societies in Britain. From time to time both C.M.S. and S.P.G. are given, sometimes with embarrassing enthusiasm, invitations to help churchpeople, especially in the United States, to fulfil their overseas Mission. The unitary systems in North America are not as monolithic as they may appear.

When we come to think about Australia and New Zealand we have a straight and very Anglican compromise in each case. Each has its own official Board of Missions as an integrel part of its national organization and both Boards, like the Overseas Department in the U.S.A. or the Missionary Society in Canada though unlike the Overseas Council in England, engage in actual overseas Mission. Yet alongside both Boards there is an entirely voluntary Church Missionary Society organization, and both C.M.S. Australia and C.M.S. New Zealand have major responsibilities for Mission outside their own country.

So we turn to England which, together with Wales and Ire-

[1] *O.M.S. Review*, Epiphanytide 1962, p. 1.

land, but not with Scotland, has the society system whereby all
the actual administration of the Church's Mission rests upon
voluntary organizations which, *whether they want to or not*
(and this suggestion we must examine closely later), must, at
present at least, retain all final power of decision in their own
hands. The Overseas Council of the Church Assembly has no
executive missionary responsibility, nor does it have any directive power for missionary work.

The Overseas Council, by its own terms of reference,[1] exists:

(a) To deepen in the Church of England its sense of corporate
responsibility for world-evangelism. (b) To stimulate support
for the missionary agencies of the Church, and to promote
co-operation among those agencies. (c) To provide a channel
of communication between the Church Assembly as repre-
senting the Church of England and the representative bodies
of other parts of the Anglican Communion. (d) To collect
and disseminate information relating to the Church's responsibility for world evangelism and to co-operate as the need
arises with other bodies working in this field.

How far the Overseas Council *can*, in the nature of things,
begin to implement its own marching orders is, in Church of
England circles at least, a much argued point. For even when
the Council reaches a firm decision there are many areas in
which it has no power to implement that decision. For example,
each Diocesan Missionary Council in England, observing the
principle of the autonomy of the diocese, has power to go its
own way. The Overseas Council can only *recommend*, not en-
force. Furthermore, if some authority in England were to
produce a fiat, 'Let all the missionary societies be made one
and let that one be subject to the Church Assembly,' it is difficult to see how anyone could prevent devoted groups of
individuals immediately setting up their own ancillary organizations to promote interest and raise funds. Nor can one
envisage a situation in which no overseas bishop would be
prepared to accept such funds for his diocese.

[1]Quoted *The Official Year Book of the Church of England* (1962 ed.), p. 248.

When all is said and done the Overseas Council carries no actual responsibility. It undertakes to provide for the Church overseas none of those supplies of men, women and resources upon which that Church depends. And that lack of responsibility could lead to a spate of airy theorizing remote from what is sometimes the grim agony of realizing that unless certain practical things—like finding missionaries and raising funds—are accomplished immediately, some overseas diocese may die of inanition. When the Church overseas wants to ensure the continuance of help or to seek new help in the British Isles (omitting Scotland), it is only the missionary societies which can supply it. To those societies we must now turn.

To explain the society system is almost as difficult as trying to explain its mother, the Church of England. And one can fully understand the attitude of so many people outside the British Isles who say: 'This is another more or less amiable eccentricity of the English. It seems to work, so let us forget about it.'

Such an attitude is, in that ancient but relevant theological term, sin. For if we are Mission because we are in Christ, then any indifference to the operation of Mission—anywhere—is indifference to Christ. So we must let our loins be girded and let our lights be burning.

We begin with the deceptively simple question: how many missionary societies are there in England? If by missionary society we mean a group of people freely gathered together to advance God's work in some particular way in some particular part of the world outside their own country, the answer is that it would be a particularly complex task to number them. There might well be a hundred or so. We must illustrate.

Normally England is regarded as having eleven missionary societies because that is the number 'recognized' by the Overseas Council of the Church Assembly. But clustered around them is a large number of independent groups each with its own loyalty. If we take work in India as an example: of the eleven 'big' societies, the following work in India: S.P.C.K., S.P.G., C.M.S., B.C.M.S., C.C.C.S. and the Mission to Seamen. But in addition you have organizations like the India Church Aid Society, the Cambridge Mission to Delhi, the Oxford Mission to Calcutta, the Bombay Diocesan Association and others as well as the direct missionary work done by the Mothers' Union and the participation of the Church of England in interdenominational work such as the United Society for Christian Literature, the British and Foreign Bible Society, or Inter-Church Aid.

It looks like chaos—so chaotic in fact that it paradoxically implies there must be some reason for it, else it would have been reorganized long ago. Just why is this system tolerated? Can it be justified?

Both those questions call for value judgements which are particularly hard in the spritual sphere. But let us see if we can isolate some of the factors.

It is customary to begin examining missionary society structures by looking at their origins. Historically one can find more than ample justification for these societies. If they had not come into being, the missionary work of the Church of England would never have begun and there would have been no Anglican Communion. The whole Anglican Communion is the fruit, under God, of the Society system. It is as simple as that. But historical justification may have little relevance to the present—and even less to the future situation and such must be our concern. But there is one historical point which we dare not omit. It is the fact that over the years these societies have, often unwittingly, acquired their own loyalties and their supporters have proved that they are prepared to make real and costly sacrifices because of those loyalties. If it were now to seem right to liquidate these societies it would be essential first to build up new loyalties, otherwise the Church overseas would be grievously the loser.

These loyalties, it must be noted, come in two quite different kinds. There are those which arise from some sort of human affection. For example, people who have worked in India but are now retired will probably have a particular loyalty to a society especially concerned with India. That is a filial *pietas*, a devotion to a country which provided them with a living, which received them as friends; and it cannot but be good. What is much more difficult to assess is the Society loyalty which arises on grounds of ecclesiastical partisanship. Historically speaking, such partisanship has been responsible for the birth of some societies. But can it be a good thing to carry such birthmarks for ever? Especially when the birthmarks are reproduced overseas in the form of monochrome dioceses?

This chapter is not the place to enter into the whole question of ecclesiastical partisanship. But we must observe that in the context of missionary operations it has a great strength as the source of a devotion which leads to the sort of sacrificial support which the unitary system can hardly hope to achieve. On the other hand, such partisanship can have a serious influence on the unity, and even the integrity, of missionary operations. And its problems are accentuated as overseas provinces increase in number.

There are two present facts which must be noted. In the first place, new provinces overseas do not seem to have been unduly disturbed by a bipartisan origin. The example of the Province of East Africa is cogent in this respect. The second point is that in England, missionary society relations nowadays never seem hindered by the partisan origin of any particular society. Perhaps it should be added that while missionary society staffs seem to work together undisturbed by partisan affinities, missionary society *supporters* are sometimes a lot more concerned about that facet of the truth which they emphasize.

We dare not minimize the importance of the society loyalties, if only on purely practical grounds. On the other hand, we must always be guided not by pragmatic considerations but by theological truth; and the devastating fact is that in this matter of missionary societies there are two relevant theological truths and they must exist in tension—though not in conflict. That they are *theological* truths is unassailable for they stem from the nature of God.

The first truth we have already dealt with. It is that God is a sending God and the Mission is Christ and Christ is the total Mission. The whole Church, therefore, is Mission and it can be argued that the administration of the Church's Mission must be the job of the whole Church. The Church must be its own missionary society.

The second truth is no less theologically based. While God gives to every man the responsibility of the total Mission in Christ, he does not expect any man to engage in every part of it. Each man in addition to his general vocation to be a Christian has an individual vocation which is his especial concern and in which he must be a specialist—deriving support from all his brethren and also acting on behalf of all of them. All this argument is no doubt accepted by the most rigorous proponent of the unitary system and he, if he were, say, an American, would point to the Overseas Department as the specialist agency. But there is a further stage to the argument. Implicit in the idea of vocation is the concept of freedom. A vocation can be rejected as well as accepted. However, if this freedom exists, then groups of like-minded people must be allowed to get together, if they believe God so calls them, to get on with a particular piece of work in the Body of Christ. Thus does the supporter of the society system find his theological argument.

We are left with the two equal truths that the whole Church is Mission and that groups of men in the Church must be free to associate in order to further that Mission.

We are left, in other words, with a particularly fascinating example of the tension between freedom and authority to which the first chapter in this book was given. Thus, if the Anglican Communion can solve the problem of the unitary versus the society system, it has made a real contribution to one of the basic problems of Christendom.

It is perhaps at this point that it is most appropriate to notice that, taking Christendom as a whole (though this is just a generalization and must therefore be qualified), it is probably the Catholic wing which goes for the society system and the Protestant for the unitary system. Contrary to what one would expect of a totalitarian Church with a highly developed central bureaucracy, the Roman Communion does most of its missionary work on the society system through its Religious Orders. It was not until 1622 that the *Sacra Congregatio de Propaganda Fide* came into existence, and even now it is not concerned with all Roman missions. For example, a separate *Congregatio* was established in 1917 for the Eastern Church, while such things as diocesan organization, the sacraments, the Holy Rites, and the administration of education are governed by other *Congregationes*. Furthermore, this *Congregatio* consists of a large number of self-governing and sometimes unruly missionary societies, each jealously guarding its independence from the others. Thus, the Jesuits in one place may have little relationship with the White Fathers in another, and converts through Roman missionary work may easily think of themselves as Dominicans or Franciscans, rather than Christians or even Roman Catholics.

The Romans have a very varied way of going about their missionary work. Many Protestants, on the other hand, for all their tendency to fissiparity, passionately attach themselves to the unitary principle. Baptists and Methodists are good examples.

The Anglican Communion, meanwhile, goes on with its reconciling task of embracing two extremes.

But we have not yet exhausted the lessons we may be able to draw from looking at the British system. In our considerations we shall omit the multitude of smaller organizations and draw an example from the eleven big ones. Perhaps we are forced to do what this chapter has been trying to avoid, put down a list[1] of names:

[1]This list is given in the order normally used by the Overseas Council of the Church Assembly. It is based on founding dates.

The Society for Promoting Christian Knowledge
The Society for the Propagation of the Gospel
Church Missionary Society
Church Missions to Jews; now renamed the Church's
    Ministry to Jews
Commonwealth and Continental Church Society
The South American Missionary Society
The Missions to Seamen
Universities' Mission to Central Africa
Melanesian Mission
Jerusalem and the East Mission
The Bible Churchmen's Missionary Society

The moment that list is scanned, a number of points become
evident. In the first place, a few of them (S.P.G., C.M.S.,
B.C.M.S.) are *general* societies in regard both to the nature of
the work they do and to the areas in which they work. The
rest are *specialist*. For example, S.P.C.K. is primarily concerned
to provide literature; the C.M.J. works only with one type of
person (the Jew), as does the Missions to Seamen. Then again,
there are those limited to a particular area, U.M.C.A. and
S.A.M.S., for example.

There is an important point here. The committee and staff
who are good at literature will not necessarily be good at looking
after seamen. Those who give all their time to considering how
to present Christ to the Jew cannot become authorities on the
Church in Central Africa. What is equally important is that
as long as missionary giving depends on voluntary effort, the
givers who are particularly interested in South America may
not be very keen on Jerusalem and the East. Equally, there are
those givers who want a limited, concentrated area such as
Melanesia for their efforts, while there are those who want to
be in the largest possible picture, and so turn to S.P.G. or
C.M.S.

But have we begged a question in that last paragraph?
Should the giving to missions be voluntary or should it be an
act of the whole Church? That is to say, should missionary

funds, whether disbursed under the unitary or the society system be an apportionment of a parochial or diocesan quota, or should they be the fruit of a free response to an acknowledged need?

We have to start by recognizing that in a fallen world missionary giving cannot be both voluntary and the act of the whole Church. In a perfect world there would be no distinction; but, until every member of the Church recognizes the obligation of Mission and responds by giving, a responsible decision as to choice of method is unavoidable. The existence of the apportionment system in any part of the Church does not, of course, exclude the use of the voluntary system right alongside it; but, so far, no Anglican province seems to have made a success of using both. Certainly no province has found a way of promoting and emphasizing both equally by one organization —and it has to be done by *one* organization if the case is to be fully met; otherwise it will not be the Church itself taking decisions, so that Australia and New Zealand cannot be cited as examples. Therefore, a choice has, in practice, to be made.

When an apportionment of a quota is the method chosen, it is superficially the act of the whole Church. Still, can it really be construed as such an act when at least a percentage of those who give will be totally unaware that they *are* giving? or, through invincible ignorance or lack of missionary education, actually resent any part of their giving going overseas? Even the briefest experience of working with a missionary organization reveals that such people do exist.

An apportionment system means that many people give unconsciously. Thus, they are not giving with their whole being. Their money is merely money and is not a symbol of Christian commitment of the whole personality. Such money, accordingly, will not be accompanied by prayer; and the insistence on prayer in our Lord's injunctions is at least as lively as the insistence on almsgiving.

The apportionment system is a categorical statement that Mission is the work of the whole Church. However, there can be circumstances in which it is a mere obeisance to the letter of the law, and that, so St Paul tells us, can be deadly.

While the apportionment system is open to criticism, so, at least to an equal degree, is the voluntary system. The latter depends on the ability of a missionary organization so to present a case that people are moved to respond by making resources available.

Now the missionary societies of the Church of England do not exist as mere money-raising bodies. (That is one illusion which must be rapidly and, we would like to think, finally exploded.) If they did, they would set about their jobs quite differently. Nor, let it be said, do they exist merely to recruit men and women for overseas service. As in the case of money-raising, that would put them into the class of mere 'appeal' pressure points.

The primary function of the home organization end of the British missionary societies is specialized Christian education and evangelism beamed at every section of the population, and especially at church-goers of every age, seeking primarily a response in prayer. Briefly, the object is so to present God at work in his world that people will want to share with God in his activity. Having done that—though, of course, in fact it is one single process, not two separate ones—the object is to be able to tell any person who seeks advice just how he or she can best respond. Motivation comes first, but it must be accompanied by competence to channel the response. Meanwhile, each missionary organization is carrying an accepted responsibility to aid the Church in some part of the world financially, with a sum already promised (otherwise that part of the Church cannot plan ahead) but not yet raised. In addition, it is trying to secure a certain sum to be available for emergencies—of which the Church overseas gets its full share these days—or for such natural growth as the inauguration of new provinces.

So much for the theory. Now to the facts of the English situation which arise from that theory. Again, we hasten to correct an error which exists at least in some minds. No English missionary society gets any state support whatsoever. Unlike those societies in, say Germany or Holland, no percentage of taxes can be allocated. All the money handled by British missionary societies is *voluntarily* given.

The British missionary societies have developed promotion and public relations machinery which is generally agreed to be in advance of what the rest of the British Church generally produces. There have been visitors from overseas who have found this not unimpressive when compared with what goes on in their homelands. In one way or another, the English missionary societies use every principle of education, adapt every medium of communication (visual, audio-visual, the printed word, and so on), and specialize their products to various constituencies, age-groups, educational standards, and the rest.

Now all this arises from the voluntary system in itself. When that voluntary system is further sub-divided into various societies, some of them very specialist, it gives scope for a personalization of missionary interest and activity which is of vital importance. For John Smith is not dropping his donation into an impersonal ocean, but is usually doing something about some specific piece of work and, frequently, some specific person, about which or whom his imagination has been kindled. John Smith is, therefore, able to *identify* himself with an on-going piece of God's activity far from his homeland; and identification lies at the heart of the whole principle of incarnation. John Smith consciously and conscientiously becomes a fellow-member with someone he may never see.

The snag about this voluntary system, of course, is that despite all its emphasis on evangelism and education it fails to persuade everyone to be a John Smith. The Church in the British Isles raises an impressive amount of money for overseas missionary work each year—perhaps as much as £3 millions (nearly $9,000,000)—yet it comes from only a proportion of those who sit in British church pews Sunday by Sunday. The missionary potential of the Church of England far exceeds its attainments—which is a statement we have also heard about other provinces. That is one of the reasons why the Overseas Council exists. Yet even its best friend could not claim that this official body has been able to add really significantly to the impact of the missionary education done by the societies.

We must return to this matter of personalization. It is, of course, not limited to voluntary societies. It can be and is developed by official departments. Yet it is through the voluntary systems, perhaps because they have developed it so much more, that it shows its worst features. Prominent among these are all the difficulties about strategy.

Some missionaries, some pieces of work, are much more colourful than others. And any missionary organization has to keep an eagle eye on its educational material lest one part of the work gets over-subscribed while another starves. For when John Smith, all on fire to help God's work forward in, say, Borneo, earmarks his gift for Borneo, to Borneo it must go even if Borneo has already been satisfied. A basic principle of society work is that they are agents for John Smith, and his wishes are final. Of course the society can write to John Smith, point out the situation and suggest diverting his gift elsewhere. But even if that were good sense administratively, it would be unfortunate psychologically, and possibly damaging spiritually. When John Smith has made a real sacrifice for Borneo, he does not like it thrown back in his teeth.

The problems of strategy *inside* the missionary society are, so to speak, paralleled by problems of strategy arising from the multiplicity of societies. When an individual, or a group such as an English parish, suddenly becomes missionary conscious for the first time, there is still the problem of which society is to be the channel for action. Each one of them can put up such a good case that decision becomes almost impossible. England has made several attempts to solve this problem but none have, as yet, proved very effective.

There is also a third area of strategy where the voluntary system provides problems. If a completely new opportunity of pioneer work in a hitherto untouched area comes up, and the part of the Church responsible for that area wants help from England, to whom does it turn? Does it have to go door-knocking from society to society until someone is impressed by the power of its appeal? Thus far in England, attempts to solve this problem have gone little further than make-shift formulas. Perhaps we ought to remind ourselves that this problem is not only a matter of English missionary strategy or the society system. It has a world-wide aspect. When new work offers, someone has to decide to which provinces or country the privilege of helping is to be offered. Someone also ought to be able to suggest the sort of total effort of which that province is capable. Otherwise it is a case of 'Do all you can and I shall still need more' which is, as someone said, no way to run a rail-road. So someone has to decide not only who shall undertake new work, but also how much new work can be undertaken. Until the Advisory Council on Missionary Strategy has much greater resources for action, we do not begin to be competent to ask the questions, let alone hazard answers. Yet until there is an answer, the *whole* Anglican Communion (for we are con-cerned with nothing less) must go on relying on the grace of God and a lot of luck.

There is one more point which ought to be made while we are on this matter of strategy. The word is almost invariably used in connection with an attempt to organize most effectively the resources of what might be called 'the sending provinces'. But that is only one side of the picture. Suppose someone had the power to organize the whole Anglican world in a com-pletely logical and sagacious way. Would that power also include some prohibition on the Church in the receiving area against seeking help elsewhere? To illustrate. Suppose for example the Anglican Communion said development in South America was to be the responsibility of the Church in the United States. Would South American bishops then be forbid-den to make a recruiting and fund-raising tour in the British Isles? And if such South American bishops really were *Anglican* bishops, would they take much notice of such an injunction?

Yet, surely, it is an odd war in which every theatre makes its own unco-ordinated appeal for limitless supplies of men and money.

Do we seem to have wandered from the point of this chapter, the administration of missionary organization? We have not. For those who work in missionary organizations have to live with these problems and produce a *modus operandi*, if not a satisfactory solution. Perhaps the real joy about being on a missionary society staff is that any tendency to theorize or lose oneself in abstractions is rudely halted by immediate and pressing problems. What is to others the sensuous delight of lucubration is to a missionary staff the agony of the decision which has to be lived with. They have to travel the road even while the road is in process of being built. And, if the metaphor is not too severely strained, it keeps their feet firmly on the ground.

There is one last area in which we must record that the principle of missionary organization has a relevance. It is that of the ecumenical movement.

In the twentieth century, praise God, Anglican missionary work can be thought of only in the context of the missionary work of other Churches. This raises two quite different sets of problems. Overseas there is all that arises from the break-down of the old principle of comity, and with that we must deal elsewhere. Here, we are concerned about the relationships of the ecumenical movement to home missionary organization.

Is it easier (a) for Anglicans (b) for those other churchmen with whom they work, to maintain and increase ecumenical relations when the system is unitary or when the system is societies? Presumably, when it is the unitary system, the missionary organization is so integrated with the Church that anything it says and does commits the whole Church. Is it a good thing for the Church thus to lose what may be a valuable area of flexibility and negotiation? On the other hand it must be infinitely easier for non-Anglicans when they have to listen to an Anglican solo rather than to the chorus which is the result of the society system. Such a figure of speech might imply that the Anglican chorus in the Conference of British Missionary Societies was usually at least a little incoherent, and perhaps lacking harmony. Experience over some years now would not substantiate such an inference. What is not generally realized is the degree to which Anglican societies share not only a common mind but also each other's confidence. Once upon a time, in their childhood, they may have been quarrelling siblings, but now they have grown up. The degree of direct, personal co-operation which goes on between them would probably alarm any gouty backwoodsman who was convinced that any diminishing of the society system would jeopardize salvation. And there are such.

The Anglican societies, then, have very much of a common mind before they go to meet with Protestant missionary societies. But they do not have a common regimentation. Accordingly, S.P.G. may pursue a policy which C.M.S. cannot support and U.M.C.A. deplore, while B.C.M.S. would want to go much further. Any combination of initials may emerge from the Anglican ingredients at a Conference of British Missionary Societies session. Probably there could be no better exposition of Anglicanism to non-Anglicans. The interesting thing is that when such society differences do occur they never harden into principles. You may be reasonably sure that any society combination at one meeting will not resemble the combination at the meeting before or the one after. Are we to hang our heads in shame that there is no Anglican party line in such matters? Or shall we admit that even a small part of the truth is bigger than all of us?

There is one aspect of Anglican co-operation with other Churches in mission, however, which remains a stubborn puzzle. You cannot co-operate in ecumenical mission without at some stage being asked to put down money. For example, you may be asked to help provide funds for an ecumenical literature project. Now there are at least two separate problems for the British set-up here. In the first place, there is a specifically Anglican organization, S.P.C.K., which exists to provide literature. Like every other organization it is woefully short of resources. Can you then feed funds into an ecumenical project for literature at the expense of your own Anglican organization? In the present climate of ecumenical emotion many people would find it easy to give a categorically affirmative reply. But the second question operates at this point: if Anglicans have given, probably sacrificially, to an Anglican organization presuming it to be for specifically Anglican work, can some committee decision override the donors' wishes and apply their gifts to ecumenical work? And if a society takes such a decision, is it then being a handmaid or a mistress? Is it serving the Church, or is it being its own final authority?

This problem, presumably, does not arise when a unitary system is supported by a Church-decided apportionment, for that same Church takes its ecumenical decisions and the missionary organizations work in the light of those decisions.

In all these matters we are like a business man who has to decide in what sort of plant his operations can best be carried on, but, while the decision is being made, production has to continue. In this chapter we have looked at the possibility of working in one building, and the possibility of using a whole cluster. Both have much to commend them and much to agonize about. So, before he attempts to decide on the external structure, the businessman goes inside to discover just what strains and stresses the works suffer day by day. He may also find the drains smell.

We have not tried to solve anything in this chapter. Rather we have tried to expose some of the facets of the problem. Through what sort of organization can the Anglican Church fulfil the Mission which God has laid upon the whole Church but which God has left every man free to reject?

Or is 'organization' the wrong word altogether? Douglas Webster, who shares the joys and panics of such a society staff (C.M.S.), has a thought-provoking word to say:

Curiously enough, organization does not seem to worry God anything like so much as it worries some of us. God has always condescended to use his Church despite its sins and follies and he appears to be more indifferent to administrative anomalies than some of us. There was precious little organization or planned strategy in the apostolic Church, yet what it accomplished was not negligible. Even its first effort after tidiness, the election of Matthias to fill the place of Judas and so bring the number up to twelve, seems to have been misconceived and mis-timed. When the moment came God chose Paul. The complete and tidy college of twelve had not accepted their calling to a Gentile mission. The obedience of one apostle was of greater significance than the organized life of twelve. There is not a scrap of evidence for believing that the early Church was centralized, either at Jerusalem or anywhere else. Once it became missionary, it could not be centralized. Paul and Barnabas were commissioned not from Jerusalem, or by the twelve, but from Antioch, and by the laity. That is how the greatest missionary movement of all began.[1]

Yet, we cannot forget that Paul did find it necessary to report back to the Church in Jerusalem; and there was at least enough inter-Church organization for the 'younger Churches' to know that the parent Church in Jerusalem was in need and to enable them to take up a collection on its behalf.

So the debate on missionary organization continues and *must* continue. God has clearly put his treasure into earthen vessels which are woefully inadequate. Yet throughout the Bible the image of the potter is a good one. He is the man who spends loving care making earthen vessels as worthy as possible.

We must go on agonizing.

---

[1] *Missionary Societies: One or Many?* (1961), p. 7.

5

The Administration of Mission: Day by Day

THE LAST chapter indulged itself, inadequately and perhaps even frustratingly, in trying to see the principles of the structure of missionary organization. In this chapter we are going to look at some of the heart searchings which are the day by day preoccupations of a missionary organization staff.

Once upon a time these problems were a relatively simple question of relationships with individual mission stations sparsely dotted around the world. Today they are immensely complicated by the—right and proper—assumption of adulthood as provinces come into being. The whole question of the relationship of a missionary-sending organization with the receiving province is an exceedingly complex one. Clearly, insofar as such words have meaning in a Christian context, the receiving province or diocese is to be autonomous. The sending organization is therefore to be a servant. But does that mean it must obey, unquestioningly, the behests of the province? Is it to become a mere automaton, or is it to enjoy a relationship of mature sharing? The Christian concept of servanthood is something far removed from the pagan concept of slavery.

It is probably the experience of most sending organizations that a mechanical response to the requests of a province would be an easier relationship than responsible servanthood. To do so would be for the sending organization to cast all onus on the receiving province and to absolve itself from all real responsibility; but that is hardly mature.

The relationship, then, of sending organizations to a receiving province is a difficult one. And it is made the more difficult by the fact that the sending organization is usually the parent, or at least the midwife, of a receiving province. How then can we begin to assess the relationship? Perhaps the parent and the teenage child is the easiest analogy. At what stage does the parent treat the teenager as mature? The answer, surely, is that there is no one answer. In some areas of his life the sixteen-year-old must be adult, making his own decisions, making his own mistakes. In others, he must still depend upon his parents. All the books in the world are not going to solve all the problems for each individual parent with each individual child—for each child, even in the same family, is different. The wise parent accepts the fact that there is no easy recipe.

In the same way we must accept the fact that no formula will be devised for the relationship of a sending organization to a receiving province—except the formula of love. And the essence of love is that each partner should be as complete, mature, and responsible as the other. This calls for two-way consultation, two-way planning, and two-way sharing. Each partner perhaps has equal difficulty in the orientation process.

Against this background we turn to the day by day preoccupations of a missionary organization staff. There are two apparently conflicting preliminary statements. The first is that, whatever the structure and ethos of a missionary organization, whether unitary or society, I suspect that some, perhaps most, of the day by day problems, and even their practical solutions, are the same. The second preliminary statement is that however much anyone may think himself into another situation, he can rarely get away from the influence of his own. There is a point in the story of the two men who leaned on a fence watching some sheep. 'Jake,' said one of them, 'I guess those sheep been sheared.' The other thought hard before replying, 'Yeah. I guess so. One side leastways.'

For the most exciting years of my life I have been allowed inside the S.P.G. family. The reader can keep that in mind as he comes to decide whether what follows has any value. He can also keep in mind the fact that S.P.G. is being used here as the type of a missionary society. The basic truths are the same for all the Anglican societies.

There is a general assumption that any organization has its own self-perpetuating institutionalism which facilitates decision-taking about problems. After all, says the bystander, S.P.G. has been active in this field for more than twenty-six decades. It is bound to have established its own way of doing things. It is bound to have a party line, a formula ready to apply to any situation.

The Society, of course, does have its laws and by-laws. It couldn't exist without them. Yet when all these are added up, they fall far short of a party line. There just isn't any blue-print to which one can turn and apply the formula without further thought. When a committee meets at S.P.G., one frequently gets the impression that this committee is a reservoir of 260 and more years of cumulative experience. What the Society did, for example, about the missionaries at Boston, Mass., when the inhabitants had a tea party there, is somehow remembered and becomes relevant when a decision has to be taken about missionaries in some emerging African or Asian nation today. Yet that strange sort of group memory has somehow not become the parent of a series of habits. Each contemporary problem is seen as being contemporary, and the possibility that an ancient good has become uncouth is never forgotten.

There is another word in that last paragraph which must be picked up: self-perpetuating. It is my sincere conviction that this word does not apply to any institutionalism which S.P.G. may have acquired. Has the time come when S.P.G. should be moth-proofed and put into its own archives? Is God now calling us to liquidate S.P.G. and merge its insights and its work into some new organization, perhaps one central English missionary set-up, perhaps indeed one central missionary pattern for the whole Anglican Communion? Has an Anglican Executive Officer been called into existence for just such a purpose? What is the Spirit saying to the Church through Bishop Bayne? Perhaps one central missionary pattern for the Anglican Communion must never be our goal. Certainly we are far from its attainment. But that provides no excuse for the casual way in which relationships between Anglican missionary-sending organizations are at present maintained. Members of the staffs of such organizations enjoy warm personal friendships. But they have never all got together for the dialogue and exchange of ideas which the present circumstances of a contracted world (not to mention the urgency of the Mission) demand. There is surely room for immediate development here.

Further than that I am not, for the moment at least, trying to answer these questions. I am just saying they are lively ones at S.P.G., and the way they are asked and argued betokens an organization which is ready to cease on the midnight hour if it becomes clear that God wants to work some other way.

I make no further apology for writing this chapter from inside S.P.G. House. Perhaps, however, I ought to make one further prefatory explanation. In the course of its history, S.P.G. has been the handmaid of the Church in thirty-eight widely scattered nations. Today, the Church in some fifty dioceses looks to it for regular support, and many more make an occasional call upon it. Now if you extract the 'settled' dioceses of the British Isles, North America, Australia and New Zealand from the total of the Anglican Communion you will find that fifty is a very high proportion of what remains. That means that a very large proportion of the 'missionary' part of the Anglican Communion is regularly telling its hopes and fears to S.P.G.

Some readers will by now have said, 'Ah, this is Morgan up to his old game of S.P.G. trumpet-blowing.' That, for once at least, is not the case. That last sentence of the last paragraph was written to establish the point that only rarely can S.P.G. have a formula which is universally applicable in its work. The circumstances of Tokyo and Trinidad, of St Helena and

Singapore, even of Madagascar and neighbouring Mauritius have relatively little in common. Few generalizations are true if they include all the diverse areas. Yet S.P.G. is committed to involvement with all those places and more.

What sort of involvement? Unless S.P.G. can continue to find men (and in this chapter that is a general term which includes women) and money, the work of the Church in those places must falter. That does *not* mean the local Church is doing nothing about self-support and self-propagation. Were that the case it would be beyond help. It just means that, as at present organized, at least, it would have to accept retrenchment rather than advance if S.P.G. suddenly disappeared without adequate replacement.

We have come to the question which is the hub of this chapter. If the local Church overseas is thus dependent upon S.P.G., what sort of relationship exists between the two entities? Does he who pays the piper call the tune?

Lest those questions be lost in the general flurry of words may we ask the reader to look at them again? Once upon a time, when missionary work was a matter of collecting a few hearers under a banyan tree, they may have been unimportant. Today, when those Churches are subject to a thousand secular as well as ecclesiastical pressures of self-realization, and when adult and responsible relationships are so eagerly sought on all sides, they are among the most important questions in this book—and perhaps the hardest to enunciate clearly, let alone answer.

S.P.G.'s principle in this matter is easily stated. The Church on the spot is mistress of its own household, employing its own staff and paying them, assessing its own priorities and the methods of approaching them, and then communicating its needs to S.P.G., which endeavours to meet them. Missionaries sent by S.P.G. are servants of the local Church, not of the Society.

In this life, the white horse of principle must be yoked with the black horse of practice, and the charioteer, however talented and experienced, finds his two steeds sometimes refuse to keep in step.

Before we lose ourselves in a jungle of metaphors let's over-simplify the whole situation by assuming for the moment that S.P.G. supports only one diocese—dare we call it Brayland?

The Bishop of Brayland is an able and godly man, so devoted to his diocese that he rarely takes leave. He finds his diocesan work so absorbing that he seldom gets right down to the bones of the wider world situation. His diocese is an island in a great ocean and is now in process of being taken over by a Left-wing government. The Bishop has on his hands a full-scale population problem, not only in terms of expanding numbers but also in new patterns of living, new housing estates around a new industrial area, and so on.

For eighty years or so, S.P.G. has supported Brayland, sending a steady flow of priests, teachers, doctors, nurses, and a block grant of several thousand pounds a year as well. Brayland is one of the places that S.P.G. home staff have found it easy to publicize, so the Church public in the U.K. know quite a lot about it.

The Bishop of Brayland notes the changing pattern of his diocese and begins to work out the way to tackle it. That new housing estate built where there was jungle till recently: it needs a priest and a house for him to live in. Let him get started and he will gather round him people who will build a church. But their children will need education so a school must be built. And a hospital too. It would also be useful to have a woman social worker and some Christian literature for free distribution. So the Bishop talks to a local builder who tells him the rough cost of house and so on. The Bishop meets the Prime Minister of Brayland who is most friendly (he was educated at a mission school) and persuades the Bishop that a school is a real priority and the government hasn't any money at the moment and the school building could be used for church services and so on.

So the Bishop of Brayland decides a school must head his

list of requests to S.P.G., thinking perhaps that if he doesn't get in soon, the Romans or Methodists or someone will beat him to it.

Now when S.P.G. gets that list, if it is going to work meticulously to its principles, it will see that the first sum allocated will be for a school. S.P.G., however, happens to have heard of the Bantu Education Act which robbed the Church in South Africa of all its schools. It has heard, too, of what happened to schools in Ceylon or Brunei, and what threatens to happen in many places. It has learned, too, that in some of the Muslim countries Christian teaching becomes increasingly difficult in Christian schools. S.P.G. also has noticed from the newspapers that the expectation of life of a Prime Minister in a newly emerging country is not always a good insurance risk. The present holder of the office may be a close and reliable friend of the Bishop's; but his successor?

In other words, while the Bishop of Brayland has, quite rightly, been devoting himself to doing God's work on one island, S.P.G. has been accumulating a world-wide picture. In that context some of Brayland's priorities may look a bit precarious. Should the Society therefore begin to strain its principles by arguing with the Bishop? It must be remembered that the money involved in building Brayland's school does not really belong to S.P.G. The Society is merely the steward, handling it on behalf of many people who have made real sacrifices to provide it. When they are told their money has gone to build a school which, from their own newspaper reading, they judge to be a pawn to fate, they are going to lose confidence in S.P.G's stewardship. The result is that the next time the Bishop of Brayland or any other bishop asks for money, however cogent and right the request may be, it may not be forthcoming.

There's another point. The Bishop of Brayland has not been there very long, he has not had occasion to build many schools, and he may not have realized that the capital cost of construction is not the end of the matter. The building has to be maintained and, probably for some years, at least a proportion of the cost of salaries must be found. If S.P.G. accepts the commitment of a school building, it is accepting a moral commitment for a future recurring grant—which will probably recur until the day the government takes the school over. Is it right to accept a capital cost until you can be sure of getting the means to meet an annual grant?

To return from the land of parables to Tufton Street, home office of S.P.G.: someone *has* to take a decision about the priorities of a diocese. It would be very un-Anglican to suggest that all bishops are always infallible. So there occur those agonizing discussions in S.P.G. House—shall we promise a priest's house or a clinic, a school or a church?

Why, it may be asked, is not the money given to the Bishop and the responsibility left to him? There are several answers. In the first place, the giving of money is not the vital thing. The all-important thing is to ensure that it is possible for human beings to do God's work in a given situation. Christianity is not the religion of a balance sheet but of persons in the Person, proclaiming God to other persons. Recruitment is the heart of a missionary society's work and is its most sensitive promotional problem. Raising money is an easy matter compared with being the channel through which vocations are heard and accepted. The basic assumption that *everyone* can give money, even if only in small amounts, is a fair one, and publicity can, accordingly, be designed to have a universal appeal. If, however, recruitment appeals are general and forthright, they can be spiritually dangerous. By their nature they call only for people with specialized gifts and qualifications. They can, accordingly, be frustrating and harmful to those who are moved by the appeal but know full well there is simply nothing they can do to respond in person. Again, a recruiting appeal has to be very careful to avoid becoming a press-gang bludgeon used to beat people into a queue for the first boat for Africa. It must do nothing to diminish the *free* response of the recruit. God does not want slaves, even if the enslavement is the result of a sincere attempt to express the Church's need. To illustrate from an extreme example: it would be wholly immoral to use subliminal advertising to recruit Church workers.

In one way and another, recruitment is a much harder problem for a missionary society than money-raising. It is something which, perhaps inevitably, proceeds unevenly. There seem to be times when not a single medical recruit, for example, is in sight. What happens if at such a time the Bishop of Brayland says his first overall priority is a hospital? Even when he is told no doctors are in sight, he replies, 'I am sure if we build the hospital, someone will turn up. We must have faith.' Who takes the final decision about the allocation of money then?

Then again, there are the whole series of problems which range round the nature of the people to whom home promotion is going, and the implicit contracts which the organization creates when it accepts their money.

The Bishop of Brayland may be entirely right when he says that above all he wants the money to build a house for a Religious Community in his diocese; that it could be a power-house, etc. Nevertheless, the home end of the missionary organization may know that at that moment, at least, such a house will be the last thing to raise a flicker of interest, and, therefore, the last thing to secure any response. Is the Bishop of Brayland to be told he must, for the present, forget his monks and nuns and provide baby food instead because it is easier to raise money to feed starving infants?

Relevant to all this, too, is the capacity of the Bishop of Brayland to change his mind. Let us suppose that in May he says his priority is an agricultural training centre. The missionary organization says yes and promptly sets about finding the wherewithal. It gets, perhaps, a hundred parishes enthusiastic. And they start sending in their money, carefully designated for this agricultural centre. Then Brayland gets a hurricane which leaves all its churches battered, or the Brayland government suddenly starts building new housing estates all over the country, and they all want new churches. 'I must postpone my agricultural centre,' the Bishop says. His decision may be the right one, but explaining it to a hundred parishes in the U.K. and persuading them to redesignate their gifts is not easy; nor does it help to build confidence for the future. Any more than it helps if, in May, the Bishop of Brayland says his agricultural centre will cost £20,000, and by the time work has properly started on it, he finds his estimates were wrong, and the real cost is nearer £100,000. 'We have begun it, so we must finish it,' he says; but the missionary organization which must go to its public and say, 'We said it would cost £20,000, but it needs five times that,' cannot expect a welcoming reception.

No doubt the friendly critic has been murmuring all through these last paragraphs; half these problems would not occur if the Bishop of Brayland were more careful before reaching a decision, and if he took that decision in fullest consultation with his diocesan council.

The friendly critic is probably right. But (a) the other half of the problems would still occur, and (b) the diocese of Brayland may be one of those dioceses which has not yet got a Diocesan Council; or be one of the dioceses—they do exist—where the Diocesan Council has not met for ten years or so.

Underlying the principle that the Church on the spot plans and directs, and the missionary organization supplies the resources, are the assumptions that church leadership on the spot really is competent to decide, and that the situation will not rapidly change and thus invalidate decisions.

Neither assumption is safe. So a missionary organization *could* be faced with a situation of intolerable gravity. It could have been supporting a diocese for many years and then find that in recent years the diocesan leadership has for some reason lost its grip. If that diocese is in any way dependent on the missionary organization for its existence, is the organization to go on sending grants, knowing its money is being largely wasted, but, thereby, a very ugly situation and, perhaps scandal, is being concealed? Or—and this *could* be the only alternative—is it to withdraw its support and thereby, to all intents and purposes, liquidate a whole Anglican diocese?

We have described an extreme example. Yet it is by no means an impossible example. It can certainly occur in many less savage forms. For example, what is to be done with the diocese which has evidently got so used to depending on a missionary grant that it is doing little to become self-supporting and thus release missionary money to go to new pioneer work? The deprivation of pioneer work is bad enough but the condition of the continually grasping, but continually static, diocese is even worse. Clearly that diocese needs shock treatment. But *who* applies it? And *who* takes the decision?

Fortunately, the sort of diocesan leadership envisaged in the last few paragraphs is rare. The Holy Spirit does seem to take an interest in most Anglican bishops. Still, not only the bad ones present problems. What, for example, is to be done about the very good one who sacrifices his holiday to making a working tour of England? Because of his patent devotion and his attractive personality, he ends his leave with a swarm of new recruits and a bagful of money to support them. There is no question of there not being enough work to occupy them fully in the diocese to which they are going. There is work in plenty. The next diocese to that one, however, probably has identical needs and identical opportunities. Its bishop is a godly, hardworking man, but he does not have the colourful personality and he chose to spend his holiday improving his grasp of the local language and culture. His diocese has only a tenth of the missionary staff and resources that his neighbours have.

Those two bishops—and they occur in more than one part of the world—provide many puzzles for missionary organization staff. Such staff are led, inevitably, to ask what is a bishop and what is his function. That is potentially a pasture of lush verbiage in which, for the moment at least, we are not going to roam. We are going to pause to ask a question which more rarely gets asked.

What is a diocese?

The *Oxford Dictionary of the Christian Church* tells us that a diocese is 'in ecclesiastical use, the territorial unit of administration in the Church. It is governed by a bishop with the assistance of the inferior clergy. . . .' The definition goes on to tell us of divisions into parishes, rural deaneries, and archdeaconries, and it is at that point that the word seems to become slightly fictitious in some parts of the Anglican Communion. Certainly there are areas where the English image of a diocese is grossly misleading. There are few dioceses in Africa or Asia which can boast of an idyllic cathedral close dotted with pigeons and canons, all of them going the same way of a seemingly cloistered life.

The grim fact is that you can find Anglican dioceses where the total clergy, of all races, consists of a bishop and two or three priests. As these words are being written, there is even a diocese which has one bishop, one priest and one deacon (who, I suppose, would have to be called Archdeacon if they insisted on having the usual diocesan structure and nomenclature).

You can also find whole Anglican dioceses where the total financial budget from all sources falls far short of the budget of many an English or American parish.

Is it possible that we Anglicans have intoxicated ourselves with our own verbosity and given grandiose names to very ungrandiose things? The question is important. For some of these dioceses—Gambia and the Rio Pongas, or the Windward Isles, for example—have no other Anglican diocese contiguous with them, and they have to look a long way before they can find the sustenance of fellowship.

Both those examples cited are in existing provinces; but to say that is not to solve the problem. It is merely to raise a whole lot of awkward questions about what is a province, and how far some of our existing Anglican provinces have any provincial entity or personality. The West Indies became a province as long ago as 1883, but how often can they have a Provincial Synod or any other occasion for getting to know each other and building a corporate consciousness? Until recently at least, if not still, it has been easier for the West Indian bishops to meet in London or New York than in their own province.

There are many problems about the whole concept of a province, but this chapter is not the place for them. What does concern us here is the relevance of this business of a province to missionary organization staffs, day by day. If the diocese of Brayland were part of a closely knit, actively conscious province, where each diocese knew and understood both the hopes and the fears of each other diocese, the Bishop of Brayland could go to the missionary organization with a list of needs which rested not on the judgement of a tiny coterie out of a whole province. Thus would each bear the burdens of all, and each share the expense of all.

Now there *are* already places where this is happening. South Africa is among the most notable of them. There are also places where attempts to attain this co-ordinated approach have done little more than expose the difficulties involved.

Not long ago the bishops of a certain province met. They all knew that the main item on their agenda was to work out the relative needs of their dioceses and present them jointly to the missionary organizations involved. It was a wholly admirable aim, and each bishop had given the matter serious consideration and prepared all his facts before going to the meeting. When each detailed his needs to the rest, however, they found they were all saying the same thing, and it was impossible, with the best will in the world, to present a joint picture of relative needs, listed in an order of urgency and importance. The province failed to do so. Yet missionary staff are *forced*, day by day, to do this very thing; otherwise, the whole effort grinds to a halt. The staff do not *want* to take decisions about priorities as between dioceses. Yet someone has to—and also has to live with these decisions when they have been taken.

The whole process of taking decisions is precisely what we mean when we talk of the relationship between a missionary organization and the Church. It is also what we mean when, in the Anglican context, we speak of Church to Church relation-ships.

Implicit in this question is the whole idea of the autonomy of a Church. The moment we think about the meaning of the word autonomy, we realize it can have no real meaning in the Body of Christ which is one Body throughout the world. No member can cherish a narrow self-identification, remote and independent, if only on purely theological grounds. Equally, in the twentieth century, no member can live in isolation, if only on practical grounds. After all, the Church in Jerusalem did not live independently of the Church in Corinth; and, as we note elsewhere, it was only when the Seven Churches of Asia were complete and integrated that the total vision was granted to them.

When we talk of Church to Church relationships, we are not talking of politicians negotiating with each other, or war-lords probing weaknesses in each other's strategy. We are talking of members of Christ, each of whom is *equally* dependent on the love of God and subject to the judgement of God. In the light of that, relative financial strengths become irrelevant, and so does talk of autonomy. Our concern must be the realization of mature and responsible partnership in the common task which God has laid upon us. Africans are as responsible for the Mission of Christ in London as Englishmen are for the Mission of Christ in Lagos. Neither is strong enough to go it alone. The fact that what Africans bring to the common task is different from what Englishmen bring to the common task is immaterial in this particular context. What is relevant is that each has equal responsibility. And God can, if he wishes, make more of the prayers of an African widow than of the munificent gift of an English millionaire.

Nevertheless, we dare not minimize the fact that in this world the Church cannot carry on without resources of money and manpower. Some parts of the world have greater reserves than others. They, therefore, have a greater *practical* responsibility. The problem is to fulfil that practical responsibility without, intentionally or unintentionally, consciously or unconsciously, splitting the world Church into Dives and Lazarus divisions. No one has yet evolved a formula for that.

Theologically, no Church can be autonomous. Equally, as long as there have to be missionary organizations—and this applies as much to the unitary as to the society system—the Church overseas simply *cannot* be autonomous in practice. It must permit someone else, at least from time to time, to speak and act on its behalf.

An historical example will serve to illustrate—and we choose something from the past, not because there is any lack of contemporary examples, but because it may be less embarrassing. The Church in South Africa has always spoken very clearly about *apartheid*. Back in 1953-54, the subject of racial segregation was for the first time making a major impact on the British public. At S.P.G. it was well known that some major publicity campaign would sooner or later be called for, and the Society had prepared a range of literature and even taken it to proof stage. The Church in South Africa, however, still hoping to prevail upon a government obsessed with *apartheid* principles, kept saying to S.P.G.: 'Hold all your material; to release it now could prejudice negotiations for which we still have some hope.' Meanwhile, the people of England were clamouring to S.P.G.: 'You say you send our money to South Africa. Give us some guidance, then, about all the *apartheid* news in our papers.' The Society had to resist such requests and appear foolish, or at least unprepared, in the process. As it happened, before the English clamour had reached breaking point, the South African government had taken brutal and irrevocable steps, and the Church in South Africa, deprived of hope of negotiation, asked S.P.G. to go ahead with its campaign (which, incidentally, resulted in many thousands of extra pounds for the Church in South Africa).

Had S.P.G. held its material much longer it would have lost the confidence of many English churchmen, and the Church throughout the world would have suffered accordingly. What, exactly, is the right course to take in such a situation? How far, for example, can a missionary organization go in giving its constituency a picture of the political context in which the Church overseas works? Remember that any such picture inevitably involves political judgements. Should the missionary organization send every scrap of its material to the overseas Church concerned before it publicizes it? Since news is so ephemeral, and it is urgently desirable to catch the public eye at a moment when a particular situation attracts secular headlines, how far is it possible to refer our publicity material to the Church overseas? Again, referring back to an earlier part of this chapter, is the Church in a particular place, with its sometimes insular experience, necessarily the best judge of how a situation should be presented to the people of a home constituency? Related to that comes the question: if a missionary organization knows that a certain course of action has in the event proved useless in one area, with what degree of insistence can it warn the Church in another area if a similar course of action seems probable there?

In all these matters, no doubt, the intelligent reader is asking: but has he forgotten all about Bishop Bayne? Does not he come into the picture somewhere? Of course he does, and the primary hope of this book is that it may help us all to see where and how he does come into the picture; but, for the moment at least, he is one man, and the world is a big place—and fairly complex too.

We have thus far been looking at missionary organization/ Church relationships, and, in this context, they are probably almost identical with Church to Church relationships. We have perhaps established the point that the problems of these relationships do not arise primarily from any vested interests of one Church or missionary society, but from the fact that the problems are of baffling complexity. We dare not suggest—for it would not be true—that no missionary society has any vested interests. For missionary societies—like Church Synods —are only another name for a collection of fallen men. We do suggest that if once the Church were to establish the formula for the right relationships, such vested interests as there are would wither away. They exist until someone can convincingly show a more excellent way—and perhaps that echo of the verse with which Paul introduces his Hymn of Love will remind us that the only ultimate Christian relationship is the relationship of love. It is a notoriously difficult relationship to express or pursue.

There are the Church to Church relationships. There are also the relationships a missionary organization acquires with individuals and sometimes these relationships raise serious questions.

A missionary organization, whether society or unitary, speaks, and someone responds by saying 'Yes, I will go.' Inescapably, the organization has contracted a moral responsibility towards that person. If I may speak utterly personally, I am always scared when I learn someone who has gone overseas was influenced in his decision by something I said or did. I have involved my life in that person's life to a formidable degree. I have, indeed, incurred a responsibility for him. A *fortiori*, a missionary organization, whether society or unitary, has a responsibility for those whom it recruits.

However carefully the missionary organization points out to the recruit that he is offering himself to the Church overseas, and, that he is being *its* servant and not the missionary organization's, this moral obligation remains. What happens, then, if that missionary, in due course, tells the sending organization that he feels a lack of spiritual care in his new job, that he knows no one to whom he can turn for advice in the deepest matters? The obvious answer, of course, is: what about his bishop? The obvious answer, however, is not always adequate. To quote a very saintly and quite wonderful non-European bishop, whose humility is a shining Christian virtue, 'I just don't feel competent to be of real help to European missionaries in deep spiritual matters.'

No doubt there are all sorts of theological, psychological and other comments to be made about that. While some are in the process of making those no doubt true remarks, others have to sort out a given and very real problem; or they have to let it go on secreting its poisonous bile until that missionary becomes wholly septic and hardly capable of doing the job God wants done.

Canon Max Warren gives clear expression to one answer to the problem. 'The missionary, like any other Christian, needs pastoral care. In so far as his needs have been at all accurately defined (in this article) he may fairly be deemed to need some particular provision for the way. I want to suggest that those *directly responsible for recruiting and sending missionaries have as their primary responsibility, to which everything else they do is secondary, the pastoral care of those missionaries*' (italics his)[1]. Dr Warren speaks with nineteen years' experience as head of the Church Missionary Society, one of the biggest of all Christian missionary organizations, and, as things are at present, he can marshal forceful arguments in his favour. Are we able to accept this as a long term approach? Must we regard the missionary as one who gives himself only partially to the receiving Church, and always maintains a lifeline with the sending Church? A relationship—and a deeply spiritual relationship at that—with the sending Church there must always be. For it will remain the duty of the sending Church to bear up in understanding prayer any of its members who has gone out to serve God. For such a member to cling to the sending Church for his *pastoral care*, as a spiritual court of appeal, which is not available to his indigenous fellow-workers, seems at least to hinder identification with those to whom he is sent. In such a situation, the sending Church can too easily come to be regarded as a spiritual insurance policy, there to be drawn upon when other resources fail.

The problem of the degree of spiritual responsibility that a sending organization has for those it sends, and how that responsibility can be honoured without impairing the receiving

[1] *International Review of Missions*, Jan. 1962.

Church is a very real one. Its full force becomes apparent only when seen in the light of the possibility which is the logic of the Church's Mission—that African and Asian Churchmen will one day be missionaries to England, the United States, and elsewhere, at the same time and in the same way as Englishmen and Americans are being missionaries to their countries. Must the Province of, say, East Africa retain spiritual responsibility for such missionaries as will one day perhaps go from Nairobi to New York?

A similar, though not identical, problem exists for the missionary on his own far up in the hinterland, with perhaps no one within hundreds of miles to whom he can speak his own language. He can, of course, from time to time go off to the capital for spiritual refreshment, but the more devoutly he does his work, the less frequently he will want to be away from it.

Both these problems, of course, and many others are related to the question of home leave. The indigenous priest who sees his missionary brother getting six months' apparent rest (the rest is certainly only apparent; deputation secretaries see to that!) is only human. Even if he were wholly sanctified, it is not right to expose him to the temptation of envy. So the Church overseas is always puzzling about the matter of furlough. So are the missionary organizations who persuade men to go. No doubt present furlough arrangements—mostly consisting of a long period of service, followed by a long period of leave—are largely influenced by the fact that they began in days when it took six weeks to cross the Atlantic. Now that it takes six hours, ought periods of service and periods of leave to be short, and all missionaries to be carried in jet planes? It would mean that lonely mission stations would not be left for months without the sacraments. On the other hand, are sudden changes from a tropical climate to the fogs of Europe good for a missionary physically? Does he need the calm of a sea voyage to reorientate mentally? Is the additional expense justifiable when resources are meagre? The questions follow each other fast and furious. And this book does not pretend to know the answers. What worries us is that so few people are asking the questions.

An equally great worry is the quite unwarranted assumption in some places that the sending missionary organization *wants* to retain some proprietorial rights over the missionaries it sends. Again, in the kaleidoscope of Anglican missionary organization, there may be some groups who *want* to retain such rights, but they are far outside the mainstream.

It is all, of course, bound up with all the problems of terms of service: stipend, for example. Is a missionary to be paid at the rate of the country he leaves or at the rate of the country to which he goes? If he is to be paid at precisely the same level as the indigenous priests among whom he works, can he, even if he is unmarried, live at the same rate as they do? Does he need different food? Does the climate cause him to need pills or potions which local men do not need? Does he have commitments to maintain back home? Must he build up a fund against the day of his final return home when he will have to set up house again?

Just what do we mean when we speak of equality of sacrifice? What is God asking of a man who is willing to relinquish the joys of familiar scenes to go and live in some remote country? What is the effect upon the local Church and its clergy of any of the answers to any of those questions?

These are real problems because they concern real people; they concern them *now* and not in some remote future. They are real problems to British missionary organizations. They seem to be even more intransigent in North America, and the whole Anglican Communion must continue to have sore spots until they are solved. These questions, indeed, will probably become more and more serious as the indigenous ministry grows alongside the missionary. They constitute not only personal problems but a moral problem which must be the concern of the whole Church. Does equal work deserve equal pay? But what does 'equal work' mean? And how do you assess

'equal pay' in the light of a wide diversity of needs and commitments?

Then there is another manpower problem which is being
perennially argued at missionary conferences: how far should
a missionary get special training before going overseas? There
are some missionary organizations, notably the Church Missionary Society, which insist that training, including language
study, and general reorientation be given. S.P.G., however,
has a half and half policy. All non-priest missionaries get a
training period; priest missionaries rarely do. S.P.G. is not unaware of some of the difficulties which arise for a priest
missionary. Why, then, no training? The major reason is
because overseas bishops are usually insistent on getting a priest
into their dioceses as soon as possible. 'We can train him
better on the spot than you can in England' is usually their
argument. Maybe they can. Probably if the priest were given
time for learning a language and getting to know local
customs, an overseas training is better. The trouble is that overseas bishops are usually so desperately short of men that
circumstances force them to throw them in at the deep end
almost before they are past the immigration officer's desk. It
becomes clear that this matter of training will find a satisfactory
solution only when the Anglican Communion as a whole can
think the matter right through.

This chapter has resolved itself into a series of questions. I
must repeat the reason why. I have attempted to put down some
of the considerations which are constantly in the minds of the
staff of at least one missionary society as they go about their
more detailed and routine work day by day. I have spoken
throughout from the background of S.P.G., not because S.P.G.
is unique but because to me it is familiar. I trust that my col-
leagues in other English societies will permit me to repeat that
I have tried to speak for them too.

They are questions which range around the relationships of
the missionary organization with the receiving Church. We
cannot forget that they are questions as arduous and urgent

for sending Churches with the unitary system as for the societies. While to some the missionary societies would appear to retain too long their hold upon individual missionaries or particular pieces of work, to others the Episcopal Church in the U.S.A. would appear to retain too long its hold on whole dioceses; but we have already said something about that elsewhere.

To ask all these questions and supply few answers may well be a mark of gross incompetence. But I am going to ask one more question: is it possible that we do not know the answers simply because we are asking the wrong questions? Should we instead be asking God if he wants his Anglican Communion bound to a box of rules and routine? In our efforts to solve these difficulties are we inevitably exluding the Holy Spirit from our operations? Theologically, that is impossible, for he can break through any barrier. But we may be making it harder for him than is necessary.

Again, I do not know the answer. I do believe that the Anglican Communion has to wrestle as Jacob wrestled, until he saw the breaking of day. Like another wrestler, St Paul, we may find our wrestling is not against flesh and blood and the difficulties of getting things organized. It may be against principalities and powers, even in this context of the consideration of routine.

Anyway, we have no choice but to wrestle. The obligation to mission is unqualified and universal. It is an obligation to be discharged not in some future Utopia but in this restless, fallen, given situation. So I leave this questing, but I hope not querulous, chapter as it is.

6

The Family which Prays Together

A QUICK reading of the Preface to the first English Book of Common Prayer might leave the impression that a primary purpose of its compilers was sheer penny-wisdom with its possible consequent pound-foolishness. 'By this Order, the Curates shall need none other books for their public Service, but this book and the Bible: by the means whereof the people shall not be at so great charge for books as in time past they have been.'

There is, surely, sanctified common sense in a Church which can let its highest principles be associated with so prosaic a formula. For it is a Church which is aware of human weaknesses and goes out to meet them, and, in deepest truth, sublimates them. Yet such a concession to human weakness is not, in the first instance, for the sake of the people. It is for the glory of God. For the Anglican Church any strict dichotomy between 'the glory of God' and 'for the sake of the people' is impossible. Anything which really is 'for the sake of the people' is ultimately to the glory of God who loves them and desires their welfare. Anything which is to the glory of God is for the sake of the people for it magnifies him in whom alone they have their being.

The Anglican Prayer Book is in some ways a monument of this divine-human polarity. Take, for example, any of the Collects. It begins with an address to God which is a strict theological statement. For instance, the two words 'Almighty God' which begin Advent I or 'Blessed Lord, who hast caused all

Holy Scriptures to be written for our learning' (Advent II). Both are strict theological statements, the *lex credendi*. Both are acts of praise to the glory of God. Both are followed with an immediate request for the sake of men. This is the *lex orandi*. Yet there is no abrupt division between the clauses. Each Collect is an integrity. You cannot pray it without learning about God, but it also asserts that you cannot learn about God without being moved to pray.

It has been customary to suggest that the Anglican Communion deliberately formulated its beliefs in prayer rather than produced some technical intellectual statement. It would probably be true to say that finding all its theology already enshrined in its prayer life, it never felt any need for a confessional formula. Either way, the effect has been the same. Anglicans have learned that men can participate *intelligently* in the Church's highest activity. The Church's one supreme and eternal activity is the acknowledgement of God's worth in worship.

Today, Christians of many allegiances are discovering anew the centrality of the Liturgy in the day by day life of the People of God. We call this rediscovery the Liturgical Movement. In this sense, Anglicanism throughout its history has been a Liturgical Movement, with intelligent corporate worship an indispensable factor not merely to its wellbeing but to its very existence. Subtract from Anglicanism its Prayer Book and you have taken its major artery.

Artery is perhaps a particularly good image, for it is something which conveys around the body the essentials for life. The Prayer Book has done just this. It is in some ways the central mystery of Anglicanism—and for an understanding of mystery we quote Gerard Manley Hopkins writing to Robert Bridges: 'by mystery you mean an interesting uncertainty whereas I mean an incomprehensible certainty.'

When we pause to contemplate the growth of the Anglican Communion throughout the world, the puzzle is not: how did this physical expansion occur? There are many reasons, such as

Western exuberance, which help one to approach (though never really find) an answer to that. The puzzle is rather: how did certain principles of spirituality get distilled by God out of a not particularly attractive period of English history and how did these acquire the seven-league boots which have carried them across the globe? And when these principles reached remote places, how did they succeed in finding root and burgeoning as they have? How did Anglican spiritual principles become indigenized in Japan or Nigeria? For Anglicans everywhere have a character of mind and soul which is one character. Here we have in mind our accessories, like a coloured stole, or superficials, like a surplice, but deep fundamentals. These fundamentals, cherished in Anglicanism, have spread beyond Anglicanism to become the marks of the Liturgical Movement. (Not that Anglicans claim to have initiated the Liturgical Movement; rather they see it taking a pattern they have long tried, however inadequately, to follow.)

What is distinctive about Anglicanism is its spirituality and not its theology—for its theology is simply that of the Catholic Church. The miracle is that Anglican spirituality has proved that it can be transplanted completely outside the matrix of the national tradition in which it was born. It can even be transplanted a second time and survive—for example, from England to the United States and from the United States to the Philippines.

A further point. There can be no question of Anglicans being *worthy* of all this. The treasure has indeed been placed in very earthen vessels. The Englishman can hardly be seen as a particularly spiritual type. In some senses he might be regarded as much more of a germ-carrier than as one who himself feels the temperature the germ produces. This does not mean Anglican missionaries have been mere unconscious instruments in the hands of God, but it surely means they have rarely been fully conscious of the full richness of the treasures they carry.

What they have had in their hands is a Prayer Book which

distils the Bible and the Creeds, which includes the raw material of the routine of spiritual life and provides for the great occasions like marriage and death, which has its roots in the spiritual exercises of a people of long ago and yet is equal to a jet age. Never has the Prayer Book been perfect. 1549, 1662 and the other variations of history, together with all the 170 or so modifications of our day, are all found wanting. They are all subject to human fallibility and provide only a jot of what we owe to God. Yet this widow's mite has been accepted, blessed and multiplied.

The Prayer Book, or at least the principle it enshrines, is central to the Anglican Communion and is the link between Anglicans and each other, and between Anglicans and God. Yet today we have to face the fact that the Anglican Communion does not have a Prayer Book. It has a whole series of Prayer Books and a growing urge to revise them all. Since no principles of revision are universally accepted, even in theory, the result can be a galloping incompatibility issuing, in due course, in the squalor of divorce or at least in an indifference akin to separation.

Is there some evidence of an awareness of this in the pronouncements on the Prayer Book made by the last two Lambeth Conferences? Were the bishops feeling that a foundation was wobbling so it was best to argue it had never been a foundation at all?

In 1948 the bishops said (II. 83): 'The Churches of the Anglican Communion are Catholic in the sense of the English Reformation. They are Catholic but reformed; they are reformed but Catholic. The embodiment of this character is the Book of Common Prayer. It is not only an important source of Anglican teaching, it is also the means by which the Anglican tradition has been sustained.' The bishops, it is true, went on to say 'We consider the time has come to examine those features "in the Book of Common Prayer which are essential to the safeguarding of the unity of the Anglican Communion" (Resolution 37 of 1920) . . .'

Such a statement recognizes what the Preface of the 1549 Prayer Book asserts: 'There was never any thing by the wit of man so well devised, or so securely established, which (in continuance of time) hath not been corrupted.'

The bishops in 1948 recognized that revision is an abiding necessity. But they show no signs of doubt, no lack of confidence, that the Book of Common Prayer is of the *esse* of Anglicanism. Can the same thing be said about the bishops at the 1958 Lambeth Conference? Recalling that their 1948 predecessors had referred to 'features in the Book of Common Prayer, which are essential to the safeguarding of the unity of the Anglican Communion', they went on to comment:

This statement appears to rest upon the conviction that the Anglican Communion owes its unity to the Prayer Book. But our unity exists because we are a federation of Provinces and Dioceses of the One, Holy, Catholic, and Apostolic Church, each being served and governed by a Catholic and Apostolic Ministry, and each believing the Catholic faith. These are the fundamental reasons for our unity. At a less profound level, we experience a unity based on the consciousness of having a common history and deriving from a common root. Of this history, the Prayer Book in its various forms is probably the most powerful symbol. The use of its forms for sacrament and worship enables us to live the life of the Catholic Church. But the special character and quality of these forms, and the theological and liturgical principles upon which they are based, impart to Anglican worship everywhere a distinct ecclesiastical culture. This common culture undoubtedly aids the widely separated provinces and dioceses of our Communion in their task of living and worshipping in godly union and concord with each other. Only in this secondary sense can the Book of Common Prayer be said to possess 'features which are essential to the safeguarding of the unity of the Anglican Communion'.

In 1958 the Prayer Book had become a 'symbol', and the bishops were not certain that even among symbols it was the most powerful. Furthermore, it is, they say, a symbol not of the continuing life of the Church but of its history of times which are over and gone! Is it fair to detect here an escapism into something static because the immediate future has a dynamic which may be uncomfortable? Should we detect in this a perhaps unconscious unwillingness to rely too much on the Prayer Book lest it gets destroyed as a link? Is it whistling in gathering gloom, if not in the dark?

The bishops went on to say, 'Should we not do better to ask what are the features of the various Prayer Books of the Anglican Communion which are most effective in maintaining the traditional doctrinal emphasis of our worship, and in preserving that ecclesiastical culture which has hitherto informed our common life and witness?' (Perhaps it would be unfair to dwell on that word 'hitherto'. But one cannot help noticing it.) The quotation continues: 'A true and discerning answer to this question would supply a number of principles which would greatly assist provinces and dioceses in the future revision of their Prayer Books.'

The bishops further note that, since Cranmer's day, a great deal of new historical material had come to light, and much more knowledge of common worship was now available. 'Therefore we might ask what elements in the Book of Common Prayer are due to the sixteenth and seventeenth century misunderstanding of what is "primitive" in public worship, and what elements need to be substituted or added in order to make the Prayer Book services truer to the ideal towards which Cranmer was feeling his way.'

We must never forget that the sum total of Anglican bishops, even when assembled in august conclave at Lambeth, does not make up the Anglican Communion. And we cannot fail to ponder the implication of those last few words of the last quotation 'towards which Cranmer was feeling his way'. That demonstrated a proper awareness that Anglicanism never has been and still is not something which has arrived. Instead, it constantly travels. It is in a very real sense a pilgrim Church.

But it has undoubtedly relied more than any Church upon its formulary of worship.

Yet here before our very eyes, it is exhibiting a hesitancy about its Prayer Book and demonstrating that hesitancy by the plethora of attempts at revision which are currently being made. Which, surely, is one more demonstration of a divine discontent which causes it not to count itself to have apprehended but always trying, with varying enthusiasm, to reach forth.

St Paul would have fully understood such a dissatisfaction; and it might help us to see our Christian way a little more clearly if we attempt to discover the causes for it. Anglican dissatisfaction with the 'incomparable Prayer Book' springs from the tensions which are at the Anglican heart. We must retrace the Church's steps.

Toward the end of the period we call the Renaissance, *all* Western Christendom was caught up in reaction or revolution. Anglicans and Protestants were involved in the Reformation, and Rome responded both to this movement and to its own inner urge with the Counter-Reformation. Both the Reformation and the Counter-Reformation had their own excesses and violences. Anglicanism, ever since, has been steering a course between Scylla and Charybdis, a course which it prays is destined eventually to harness the immobility of Scylla with the flux of Charybdis.

What happened about men's devotional life as the stormy voyage of the Reformation proceeded?

For Protestants, there was the great return to the Bible. The supreme task of man was seen as breaking open the Scriptures. Its most obvious expression was in preaching, but we misread the signs if we forget the vast personal devotion given to the Bible and nurtured through the Bible. 'England became the land of the People of the Book and that Book the Bible,' said J. R. Green in his most quoted moment. From that we trace the vast and indeed quite immeasurable influence the Bible has had on the warp and woof of English life. No doubt continental historians have traced comparable results in the life of all the countries of Protestant Europe.

In a sense this Protestant attention to the Bible tended, until our own day, to get narrower and narrower. The broad sweep of God's dealings with his people, from Genesis to Revelation, seemed more and more to get lost. The popular preacher chose his favourite texts—often from the fiery, and not necessarily representative words of the Old Testament—and he wrestled with them through the night as Jacob wrestled with an angel; and, as Jacob did, he had his reward, for he saw God face to face. But it was a partial, fleeting view, and the hollow of his thigh was put out of joint in the process. The Protestant wrestled with his Bible and kept it before men's minds. All Christendom must be indebted to him, for, without him, we might by now have let God's Book fall into the desuetude from which there is no easy return.

Even while acknowledging the debt, or indeed as a repayment of the debt, all Christendom must remind the Protestant that in time the Church came before the Bible. The prophets thundered their message to an existing Chosen People, and St Paul wrote his letters to an existing Church at Corinth, or wherever.

While Protestants were busily and unhappily proving that even one of God's greatest gifts can make a barrier when distorted and interposed between the Father and his children, Roman Catholics were demonstrating that this same gift can be despised even by God's People. For they were making the Bible inaccessible, sometimes even forbidden, to the ordinary man.

While Protestants were learning more and more to know and love Moses and the prophets, Paul and the preachers, Roman Catholics were becoming ever more closely attached to the heroes of their past, the saints. Now the essence of sainthood is a life lived in proximity to God, a life which by definition includes a great deal of personal prayer. The open Book of Protestantism was paralleled by the inner life of the Roman

Catholic; and all Christendom must humbly acknowledge its eternal debt to those sanctified stalwarts who have written the signposts for the soul's path to God. At the same time, all Christendom must point out that those spiritual techniques could be devoted to an individualism entirely alien to the common life of the Body of Christ. All too frequently, they were.

At first sight, the Roman Catholic Church of the Reformation period appears above all to be a functioning body with common actions, even if those actions had become corrupt. After all, did not all Roman Catholics go regularly to Mass and thus share in worship with their fellows? The good Roman Catholic certainly went regularly to Mass and found lots of other people in church at the same time as himself. He did little, however, to share in a common worship. He would be entirely immersed in saying his private prayers, repeating his Litany quietly, or telling his beads wordlessly, interrupted only by a *Sanctus* bell bidding him reverence the elevated Host.

The Mass had become a priestly solo. The Bible had become a private pocket book of problems and solutions to be sorted out personally with God. Both Roman Catholicism and Protestantism had become essentially individualistic, and most of the branches were acting as if there were nothing else on the Vine.

Then, for reasons which the historians seem merely to obscure and make tortuous beyond imagination, something happened in England. Here a few and there a few began to realize that God is a Father and his children cannot live in isolation from each other, any more than they can live in isolation from him. This realization found its formulation not in a complex statement of credal facts nor in any epoch-making new theologian but in a Prayer Book. It was a realization expressed in *action* and not in definition, more concerned with what we are and what we do than in any fumbling attempts to reduce the Majesty of God's glory to a set of characters on paper. And concerned, too, that what we do should be the highest and best, should be worship. Thus was born the Book of Common Prayer whose Preface writer alleged one reason for the birth was that 'the people shall not be at so great charge for books as in time past they have been'. (The angels must smile at the devious ways that those made a little lower than themselves become crowned with glory and honour.)

What that Prayer Book set out to offer was a form of worship which was both biblical and corporate, with the material for real personal devotion still available for private use. The Epistles and Gospels, the daily readings, the scriptural basis of all its acts encouraged—compelled—men to meditate on God's Word, but now the words which made up the Word could be seen only in total context and never as isolated aphorisms. At the same time, the constant repetition of public worship both inspired the content and elevated the form of private devotion. There is, perhaps, a criticism in the very success of this latter aim. For Anglicans, intoxicated by the beauty of the English language at its highest moment, have come to feel that God understands only one literary style, a style which inevitably tends to betray us into regarding him as our *Grandfather* who 'art' in heaven. You have to be polite to grandfathers in the hope they leave you something in their will. But that won't come till they die. Even without hope of a legacy, of course, grandfathers do deserve respect, but, generally speaking, they spend their time in reverie rather than action.

The arrival of the first Book of Common Prayer did no more than allow people to glimpse a promised land. They were a long way from setting up their homes in it. They still are. Yet this vision of the common people doing things for God in common abides.

One reason for that lies in the fact that the shapers of the Book of Common Prayer somehow saw, appreciated and retained both the insight of the Protestant Reformers and the insight of those they would reform. The Book of Common Prayer is an attempt to make worship utterly biblical, and at the same time provide a treasury of prayer and worship which can be used almost as much in private as in public.

It is *biblical*. But this word biblical calls for explanation, and the explanation demonstrates that Anglicanism is neither Protestant nor Roman. For the Protestant, the Bible means the Old and New Testaments and no more; for he repudiates the Apocrypha. For the Roman Catholic, the Apocrypha is on a par with the Canonical Scriptures. The Anglican finds a compromise. For him the Bible is comprised of the Canonical Books of the Old and New Testament, but he also says of the Books of the Apocrypha, 'the Church doth read them for example of life and instruction of manners; but yet doth it not apply them to establish any doctrine'. The Prayer Book is biblical. In its regular services, whether the Eucharist or the daily offices, and in its actions for special occasions. Baptizing, marrying, burying, all are occasions of being reminded of God and what he is doing, through Holy Writ, as well as of receiving the ministrations of the Church.

The more one looks at the Prayer Book, the more one is convinced that the Church never misses a chance of proclaiming God. The bride on her day of glory is reminded that God in Christ went to a wedding in Cana of Galilee; the mourners at the last rites are reminded that Christ, too, died, and death has never been the same thing since; and it is all done without trace of mawkishness or sentimental human self-regard. It is just a quiet and convinced statement of the fact of the death and resurrection of God the Son without which our intercessions and praises would be vain rumblings.

The Prayer Book is the plain man's *précis* of the Bible. It is also, in its own right, a course of devotion. The Anglican Liturgy is a vernacular liturgy, and when you hear it year by year, you not only have more chance of learning something of its meaning and adding intelligence to your other faculties in worship; you also find that its rich phrases, in your mother tongue, soak into your being, providing a treasury from which gems can be taken—or, indeed, come automatically—as the soul seeks spiritual expression.

There is also one other great characteristic of the Book of

Common Prayer. It did not and does not set out to provide some exciting novelty. The Preface to the first Book of Common Prayer not only pleads economy as a reason, it also states that 'these many years passed, this godly and decent order of the ancient Fathers hath been so altered, broken and neglected'. So the Book sets out to offer something 'much agreeable to the mind and purpose of the Fathers'. As evidence in support of that, we may note the way in which the three Catholic Creeds are not only doctrinal authorities but are also regularly used in worship.[1]

The Prayer Book was born of a sense of the continuity of the Church—rooted in the Bible and fulfilled in the common life of the Body of Christ. Thus the Prayer Book is not only solidly biblically based, but also acknowledges its lineal descent from the Breviaries and Missals of the Western Church. This inheritance of past centuries is something for which the whole of Christendom in our day, sometimes in actions more than in words, is showing an appreciation. The great return to the Bible in the Roman Church, the great recovery of the idea of the Body of Christ in Protestantism, each with its consequences —which we have come collectively to call the Liturgical Movement—might not have been possible had not the Anglican Communion already been guided to a Prayer Book. It is most improbable that at first it saw all the potentialities of this Prayer Book; but God did, and somehow ensured they were not lost.

The Book of Common Prayer is very far from being perfect. It is as far from its ultimate ideal as a rough sketch is from Leonardo's Last Supper. In the Church of England, indeed, the tercentenary of the 1662 Book of Common Prayer was allowed to pass without all the anniversary fanfares to which the Church is normally given. Was this due to a feeling that in 1962 a Book compiled in 1662 could hardly fulfil its own ideals? Is sonorous Tudor prose the 'vernacular' for neo-

[1] In no other Church,' says Dr Molland (*Christendom*, p. 150), 'have worshippers a similar opportunity of hearing all three Catholic Creeds.'

Elizabethan man? Is not the English Prayer Book now more a gathering place of ideals rather than their actualization? But this is a domestic question for the English and of relatively (but only relatively) small importance when we are being concerned with the whole Anglican Communion. What really concerns us here is that the Prayer Book has nurtured and does nurture ideals. It has sensed the end in its beginning. Now the Prayer Book and the mental and spiritual climate begotten through it can and must call out to the great wings of Christendom: come alongside and help us to attain to what God wants; without you neither we nor our Book can be made perfect.

It is, surely, a moment of excitement, and quite certainly not a moment for the Anglican Communion to falter and fumble, nor to fall apart in its development. The cry for revision is loud. Even in England, which in the curious conditions of Establishment seems likely to be the last part of the Church to attain revision, the voices are loud. Archbishop Michael Ramsey had hardly reached Canterbury before he was saying that a state connection must not be allowed to hinder the right desire of the Church to order its own worship. The cry is equally loud throughout the world.

The Anglican Communion has a duty to heed the situation and ensure that there is some chance that the family will remain a family even while each adult member goes his own way.

To return to the 1958 Lambeth Conference. The bishops there realized this duty of revising the Prayer Book. They made it clear, however, that they did not feel called to 'urge' all parts of the Anglican Communion to embark on revision at once; neither did they counsel maximum revision. The conservatism which kept Anglican reformers looking back to the Fathers is far from dead, and the last temptation Anglicans are likely to suffer is a desire for change for the sake of change.

'But revision,' they said (2.93), 'is nevertheless proceeding, and the movement cannot now be halted. The Committee's aim has been to try to indicate the direction which this movement should take when it has begun. We are not the only branch of Christendom to have set about this task. Both in the Roman Catholic Church and in the Evangelical Churches a similar movement is in progress. And because this Liturgical Movement has already begun to draw Christians closer to one another in thought and ways of worship, we cannot wish that our own Communion should stand aside.'

Does that mean that Anglicanism will be permitted to mark time in this matter until the ecumenical movement has disappeared in a totally united Church and all the conflicting emphases of worship have been resolved? It would be sad if that were so—and false to our vocation and history. For if Anglicans really do esteem the principles of their Prayer Book in the way they say they do, they must surely see in it one part of their contribution to the ecumenical movement. What is the connection between this Book and the ecumenical movement?

The first part of the answer lies in the fact that it is the Prayer Book which most of all has prepared Anglicans for their participation in ecumenism in a sense which goes beyond the present breadth of the World Council of Churches. For the Prayer Book has made them, so to speak, bifocal. On the one hand, it has helped them understand all the ideals and hopes of the great Roman Catholic Church. Anglicans may have real reservations about the doctrine of the Immaculate Conception, but they have a real place in their Kalendar for Lady Day, so they know what the Romans are trying to secure in such a doctrine. Anglicans may have mixed approaches to the idea of the sacrifice of the Mass, but they all constantly talk to God about a 'full, perfect, and sufficient sacrifice, oblation, and satisfaction, for the sins of the whole world'.

Similarly, Anglicans can understand the Protestants who talk about justification by faith and see in the Bible all that is necessary to salvation. Anglicans, indeed, do hold that the Bible contains all that is necessary to salvation, but they also insist on the necessity of the Church to teach what the Bible proves. Anglicans are beings who live in two ecclesiastical worlds at the same time. They can either be fellow-travellers, with all the implications that word has come to hold, or they can be living emissaries linking the two worlds.

The Prayer Book is a passport to ecumenicity, and the Anglican Communion did not have to wait until the twentieth century to see the possibilities. Bishop Stephen Neill reminds us[1] of Edward Pococke (1604-91) who translated the Prayer Book into Arabic, partly in order to commend the Church of England to the Patriarch of Constantinople, and of Isaac Basire (1607-76) of whom John Evelyn wrote, 'that great traveller ... who has been planting the Church of England in divers parts of the Levant and Asia'. Basire himself was very twentieth century in his aims: 'It hath been my constant design to dispose and incline the Greek Church to a communion with the Church of England.' There were also others at this time, but the ground was not ready for the seeds they had to sow.

Nor was the interest confined to the Orthodox world. The great Archbishop Wake (died 1737) had a quiverful of projects, including a plan 'to bring the Gallican Church to such a state that we might each hold a true, Catholic unity and communion with one another'. Wake's activities were not limited to France. He also worked hard for an understanding with Lutheran and Reformed Christians in Switzerland and Germany. The relevance of the Prayer Book to all this is demonstrated by the German translation caused to be made in 1704.

'If these many schemes,' says Bishop Neill, 'led to nothing in the way of practical and visible results, they at least served to keep alive in England the idea of the *Una Sancta*, and to make other Churches aware of that spirit of comprehensiveness which has been the lasting glory of the Church of England.'

The point we have tried to make is that the Prayer Book has a profoundly utilitarian aspect and especially when we come to think of ecumenicity. But such usefulness is always secondary to the Book's real purpose which must be always in the front of our minds. So we remind ourselves of one more Lambeth 1958

[1] *Anglicanism* (1958), p. 200ff.

quotation (2.78): 'The Prayer Book is the public expression of the worship of God in the Anglican Communion, and it is on the worship of God, creation's secret force, that all human activity depends. It is only in worship that *all* the Church can learn the will of God and receive wisdom and power to do it . . . Worship then is the first concern of the Church, and it must be the worship of the whole Church, priests and people together bringing to God every human interest and activity and problem and conflict to be taken into his will and used for his purposes.'

The effects of their Liturgy upon Anglicans are to be seen in the Anglican Communion's own particular form of piety. The Liturgy has influenced their intellectual life and permeated their culture. Even on that manward (so to speak) level, the Liturgy is a talent which we dare not bury in the earth or even allow to sink into the undergrowth. On the Godward plane, it is the expression of man's first duty and his chief end. It is something peculiarly Anglican; we must treat it as one of the reasons for our very existence and cherish it as a drowning man would hug his lifeline.

The Liturgy is vital to the Anglican Communion. So we ask some questions: Should each province have the sole right to make whatever revisions it likes regardless of the opinions of the rest of the family? What happens if the revisions of one province fall into obvious and open conflict with those of other provinces? How, in present circumstances, can provinces even adequately consult each other, let alone keep in step when revision is on hand? And, if they are kept too closely in step by any rigid authoritarianism, does this mean that indigenous Christians in, say, Africa and Asia, can never make their own peculiar contribution to Anglican worship? Could the letter of the law in this respect indeed kill the spirit?

These are real questions and we dare not leave them to the liturgical experts as if they were the specialist concern of one bit of the Church. Such experts are indeed necessary, just as an architect is necessary to good building. But the architect does expect meaningful briefing before he reaches his drawing board.

If we might strain that figure a little further, what the Anglican Communion must be is a liturgical house of many mansions; and each mansion needs to be integrated with the others—and yet preserve its identity.

There are, unhappily, several rumblings which suggest the mansions are not being carefully and jointly planned. The last Lambeth Conference had a strong desire that there should be some meeting point at which joint planning could happen. To provide that place was one of the duties added to the interminable catalogue laid upon the desk of the Anglican Executive Officer. But how is he to facilitate the dialogue which is necessary? How are revisers in various areas to gain access to a central treasury while yet there is time to use it in their own revisions. Just *what* does the Anglican Communion want to do about its Prayer Book? And just *how*?

All Christians must constantly be bothered about the quality of their worship. After all, it is one of the few things we can do on this earth which we may hope to continue through all eternity.

7

Family Ties

To WESTERN man, with his passion for organization, and his apparent conviction that nothing can work well unless you have administrative tidiness, the Anglican Communion must surely be a cogent proof that the doctrine of the survival of the fittest has little validity in spiritual matters. The last thing which the congeries of Anglican Christians can claim is any mechanical efficiency. By most natural laws, the Anglican Communion simply should not exist. Yet it does. To the question 'What holds it together?' there can be only one answer: God. And one frequently gets the impression that God must want it pretty powerfully, else it would have disappeared long ago.

Anglicans themselves, we have been at pains to point out, can claim no sort of credit for the coherence of this Communion thus far. Nor even, to any marked degree, for an awareness of that coherence. They cannot begin to claim to be worthy instruments of God in this matter. Yet perhaps there is some secret in their very unworthiness. After all, when God wanted to prepare mankind for the coming of his Son, he did not choose the grandeur that was Greece, or the glory that was Rome, but a backward, backsliding peasant people.

The Anglican Communion is so loosely knit that one constantly feels it must become utterly disjointed; so centrifugal that there is an ever-present expectation that its members will at any moment launch into separate orbits in the dimmer reaches of outer darkness, the place of gnashing of teeth.

If this appearance of imminent disintegration were merely a

contemporary phenomenon, Anglicans might have cause to start writing obituaries. The whole of its history, however, is consistent in regard to its *human* inconsistency. This book is concerned with the present situation and even more with the future, but we must spare just a moment for the past.

The Church reached the British Isles fairly soon after the Pentecostal experience, perhaps in the first century. There is even a theory—though it is not substantiated—that St Paul may have visited Britain. How the Church reached Britain, however, must be a matter of conjecture. Perhaps a Roman soldier 'gossiping' the Faith, perhaps a Celtic lead trader picked it up as he pursued his Mediterranean commerce and brought it home. Britain has no Christian founding father as, say Sweden, has an Anskar.

Then, many centuries later, came St Augustine, perpetuating a famous pun about Angles and angels, and there began the great Roman takeover which was to crumble at the Reformation. Then *ecclesia Anglicana*, a title which goes back at least to William the Conqueror, began its modern phase. The Church of England is quite certainly a Reformed Church. But it is not, and never can be, a Reformation Church.

The Church of England has a missionary history going very far back. St Boniface is only one luminary among a number of not necessarily lesser lights. In the medieval period when Western Christians lost their national identities in the greater concept of Christendom, we may be sure that many Britons played their parts in missionary work outside their own country.

The Reformation left the Church of England with no organization for missionary work. Nevertheless, English clergy went overseas, though usually to minister to their own compatriots. Thus one 'Maister Wolfall' left a comfortable home in England to sail with Frobisher and celebrated the Holy Communion for the first time according to the Anglican rite in the New World. A year later Francis Fletcher, Sir Francis Drake's chaplain, held a service in the presence of a large number of American Indians, who were reported deeply impressed by what they saw.

English authorities still gave little encouragement to such efforts. When Queen Elizabeth I gave her Royal Charter to the East India Company in 1600, the Company was permitted to have chaplains, but only on the strict understanding that their ministrations were to be solely for the Company's expatriate servants. Any attempt to commend Christ to the Hindus was strictly prohibited. Nearly two centuries later, William Carey was not permitted, as a missionary, to sail to India on a British ship or to live in India on British soil. The Danish Government seemed to have a much greater appreciation of Christian vocation, for Carey could operate freely in their territory.

All in all, anyone suffering the delusion that the Anglican Communion came into being because the British government had a consistent policy of supporting Christian missions alongside the secular arm of expansion need only consult a history book. Spanish and Portuguese explorers, soldiers, and colonists had indeed regarded it as important to build a church as a barracks, and the spread of the Faith had kept step with the spread of the secular arm. The English had been much less zealous.

The Anglican Communion cannot be attributed to British Imperial policy. Nor can it be attributed to the ecclesiastical policy of the Church of England in any official capacity. Organized missionary work from the British Isles began only when a few individuals, moved by God, got together and set up societies. Even then the official Church went dreamlessly on. For example, the whole history of the attempts made by the Society for the Propagation of the Gospel to provide America with at least one bishop in the first three-quarters of the eighteenth century is a story of vision thwarted by unimaginative authorities.

Yet by the year 1800, the first bridgeheads of the Anglican Communion had been established. A sprawling, so often apparently fortuitous, growth had produced Anglican communities in North America, the West Indies, Africa and Asia. Even then, however, the Church of England seemed to have no sort of awareness that it was being called to family life. Missionaries were going across the world; bishops were being appointed; and that was that. It was a missionary society, S.P.G., not the Church of England in any official capacity, which first made any real acknowledgement of the existence of American bishops when it invited them to its 150th anniversary in 1851 (nearly a century after the consecration of the first American bishop). And it was a Provincial Synod in Canada, not England, which in 1865 first took serious steps to combat the increasing isolation into which worldwide Anglican nodules were falling. It called for a meeting of Anglican bishops and the result was the first Lambeth Conference in 1867. The Archbishop of York and all the bishops of his Province even then disapproved so strongly of such goings-on that they refused to attend.

There are times, many times, when we bewail the Anglican Communion's lack of a sense of fellowship today. Perhaps we ought to check our perspectives and thank God for the progress that has been made, a progress that is, humanly speaking, astonishing—yet a progress which in so many ways seems unsatisfactory. So much remains to be done. More serious still, it is a progress which seems to be in jeopardy every hour not only because of secular pressures but also because of the seeming weakness of Anglican bonds. Our glance at history forces us to wonder if Anglicanism can possibly have any glue holding it together. Are the member Churches of this Anglican Communion really grafted into each other, or must one acknowledge them a very temporary agglomeration, held together for the time being by what could be a merely ephemeral sentimentality?

The historians cannot give a great deal of help with the answer. The Anglican Communion, as it now is, is in so many ways contrary to its own expectations—if, indeed, it ever had such. It might surely be inferred from historical circumstance that the Church of England would have a natural leadership in this Anglican family. Can anyone for a moment suggest that this is indeed the case? Consider such matters as

Prayer Book revision, synodical government, and stewardship.

To approach the matter from the opposite angle, can it be shown that the major features of the Church of England have been reproduced in the Churches of the Anglican Communion? Some, yes. But all, very certainly, no.

Whatever the spiritual significance of Establishment may be as far as the outsider is concerned, this is a major characteristic of the Church of England. Yet Establishment does not obtain even in the Church of England's two nearest sister Churches— in Wales and Scotland—and it remains little more than a tantalizing mystery in America or Japan. Only one diocese, Barbados, in all the world outside England is established— (even that statement could well be untrue by the time these words are read).

Establishment, of course, is a matter of circumstance rather than of theology, an outward and visible sign without a really distinct inward and spiritual meaning. If Establishment were in any sense an essential ingredient in the Anglican ecclesiastical culture, the worldwide Anglican Churches would face many problems in this revolutionary twentieth century. There are countries where Anglicanism would be more chameleon-like than the Vicar of Bray. But that is not necessary, for Anglicanism does not depend on any particular Church/State relationship. What the Church has to do is first of all to fear God and then, in so far as is consistent with the first injunction, honour the king, the president or whoever may be the symbol of government. There, however, we have expressed a principle, not a method. In its principles the Anglican Communion can be united. Methods are another matter.

Usually in life principles (when they are carefully distinguished from prejudices) are the things which unite, while it is the methods of realizing those principles which divide. All men of goodwill, whether Christian or non-Christian, European or non-European, educated or primitive, are united in a number of principles, for these principles stem from the primary elements in man's make-up. They hold as principles for example, that it is good to have some security in which personality can be developed; that it is good to be able to look forward to one's children being better than oneself, irrespective of by what canons betterness is judged. There are numerous such principles and they unite men.

It is when you come to methods that disunity comes—such a degree of disunity that it is comforting to remember that the principles are eternal, but the methods of realizing them may have a mayfly existence. Most women agree as a principle that there are occasions when it is good to have their heads covered. But the method, the particular style of hat, has little expectation of a long life.

It is its principles which are a bond of the Anglican Communion. Anglicans approach things in a similar spirit. In its local expression that spirit can legitimately take varied shapes. Anglicans have had their methods and systems. They have had freedom not only to follow them but also to form special associations of like-minded people for that purpose. This is one of the factors which has caused ecclesiastical parties to grow up in the life of the Church of England, parties which have been propagated, but fortunately—as contemporary events seem to show—not perpetuated, in the Anglican Communion. It was once customary to suggest that it was only the fact of Establishment which kept these English parties in one Church. There is no Establishment overseas but the parties have existed there; and the Church has nevertheless held these parties together without the help of this alleged political glue.

To many people, such partisan spirit as there has been in the Anglican Church has been taken as powerful evidence that this Communion is a very artificial and unhappy mixture. That is perhaps too easy and obvious a deduction. It can also be argued that the existence of these parties, contrary to what might be expected and, indeed, to all common sense, has actually been a uniting factor. For if the militant ones who have held to either extreme have had any single thing in common it has been a dogged determination not to let the other extreme take posses-

sion. The very pertinacity of the 'high' for the things which are
high, or the 'low' for the things which are low has forced them
both to stay in the same Church lest those they oppose should
win the day and mould the Church to their will.

Inevitably it must seem specious to argue that it is the very
opposition of the opposing forces which has contributed to
Anglican unity, yet such is surely the case. This conviction is
substantiated when you dissect the heart of Anglicanism, for
its nature is not to be *either* Catholic *or* Reformed but to be
both.

To a surprising degree that vocation to be both is being
realized. We talk—very rightly—of party strife as being a thing
of the past. The reconciliation between high and low in England today is an astonishing sight for anyone who has a picture
of English church life in the century between 1840-1940. Today the wolf lies down with the lamb (and I refuse to identify
either). The strange and miraculous fact is that this is not
because either party has been obliterated. Neither has lost, but
both have won, and both seem to be winning more and more;
and the whole Church is winning, accordingly.

To take but one fascinating example: that part of the world
which less than half a century ago torn by the Kikuyu
controversy is now the Province of East Africa. As clear a case
as ever could be of 'high' versus 'low', the Kikuyu controversy
seemed certain to disintegrate Anglicanism. One Anglican
bishop had felt forced to indict another Anglican bishop who
was his neighbour. Each felt that the principles for which he
stood were vital and a serious schism seemed the only possible
outcome. Perhaps had it not been for the outbreak of the first
World War this tragedy would have happened. But that war
deferred judgement on the matter and men had time to think.
By the time of the 1920 Lambeth Conference reconciliation was
possible. Today both these very different Anglican dioceses are
united in the Province of East Africa and there are those who
regard this province as one of the brightest examples of the
potential of Anglicanism. Churchmen of very diverse traditions

are proving how well they can work together. Indeed it may be the very difference of traditions which makes the province as creative as it is. And perhaps one of the most important lessons it is offering us is the value of having the whole ecclesiastical colour spectrum available when it comes to painting the true picture of the Church.

There is another aspect of this matter of high and low which must be borne in mind. It is that both high and low at their best have always been *positive* in their thinking. At moments either party may have appeared merely anxious to negate the other; but to elevate such episodes into a theory or a judgement is to equate the practicalities of polemics with what the war is all about. While both parties have from time to time descended to dog-fights, neither has regarded itself as existing for that purpose. Both have stood—and still stand—for a positive set of beliefs.

That seems a good thing. It is. But in this piebald human life it also has its weaknesses. Human nature always seems to show a more lurid interest in the negative than in the positive. Even a cursory glance at that ultimate measure of public concern, a newspaper, indicates that sin is more interesting than virtue. War is more interesting than peace. It is—or at least, history, including contemporary history, would suggest it is—easier to gear up a nation and get it united to fight against an enemy, than it is to inspire it to fight positively for its own welfare. Winston Churchill could weld the British into one nation in the early 'forties. Neither he nor anyone else had much success in that direction once Hitler became a memory.

Anglicanism is a *positive* Faith, not out to fight *against* anybody. In the long run, of course, that is undiluted virtue; but in the short term, it can appear to leave Anglicanism a shapeless lump reeling in several directions at once. The comprehensiveness of a body of people geared up to get on with a job can degenerate into a sorry compromise when the vision of the job blurs, or when the sense of urgency provided by an enemy at the gates is dissipated into a vague good intention about the future. Tomorrow, said someone, is the best labour-saving device ever invented.

Alongside this is another matter. It would be possible to imagine Anglicans as getting too polite towards each other nowadays. It is one thing for the brethren to walk together in love. It is quite another to suggest that the people you love are always right, or that being in love exalts good manners above truth. It is a good thing that Anglican opposites can be seen quite definitely as belonging to the same Church. It is quite another when family peace can be equated with domestic inertia. One great advantage of having two extremes in Anglicanism is that each has been so critical of Anglicanism. The Anglican Communion must surely be the most self-criticized Church in Christendom. As long as that criticism flows from a desire to reach God's standards and not from any carping introversion, that is a good thing.

Anglicanism is a positive faith, and therefore is creative, rather than a negative faith, and therefore destructive. Being positive and creative, it is also dynamic. That is a word which must be numbered among the casualties of our generation. It has almost lost its meaning. If we cut away the accretions, however, we get back to the idea of a force in actual operation. It is in that sense that Anglicanism is dynamic. Which means two things. In the first place it is in actual operation. You cannot tie it down and list its ingredients in the way you can for something static. Anything which is dynamic has all the exasperating qualities of life—exasperating to the analyst who finds that anything he pins down is not quite the same thing as he set out to examine. Some vital quality has disappeared up the laboratory chimney.

The second thing that a force in actual operation can be expected to exhibit is results—perhaps effects is a more modest and appropriate word. Has Anglicanism produced any effects?

In the first place, the Anglican out-thrust has taken place in the context of the total Christian out-thrust, and many of its effects are one with and, quite rightly, lost in, the total picture of Christian results. Thus, for example, Anglicanism cannot and must not claim any unique share in the impact that Christianity can be demonstrated to have had on Buddhism; or on the emancipation of women in Asia; or on the idea of democracy in Africa; or many other things.

This is not to suggest that Anglicanism has made no contribution to such things. It has. But its contribution cannot be isolated from and identified apart from the general contribution.

There are points, nevertheless, at which a specifically Anglican effect can be seen in Christianity outside Europe and some of them are things we do not want to boast about. To choose a brutal example, there are far too many Anglicans in Asia and Africa who think there is something deficient in their Faith or Order if they are not fully acquainted with *Hymns Ancient and Modern* (and not in its revised form at that!) and all that goes with such things—that peculiar garment, the surplice, for example.

In other words, Anglicanism has carried in its luggage far too many of its accidents, and undue attention to the accidents must usually be at the expense of the substance. There are many Anglicans who on visiting, say, India, are so impressed and mesmerized by a church of quite incongruous Victorian Gothic architecture that it takes them some time to become conscious of the reality enshrined inside those lancet windows, or the spirituality of the people who use those improbable pews. Neither surplice nor Gothic architecture can be regarded as positive Anglicanism but they are part of the situation as it exists.

Anglicanism, in fact, is often far too anxious to be English; and this is a drawback. Before we tut-tut ourselves, however, into a state of righteous indignation, we must note two things.

In the first place, those accidents do help to bind Anglicans together. After all, it is by the shape of a nose and a chin, the colour of the eyes and the hair, that you recognize your friend. There can be some virtue in a Victorian design, even in Japan or Jamaica, so don't let's dismiss it altogether.

The second consideration ranges round the whole problem of the indigenization of Christianity. It is a problem as complex as it is vital; and, of course, it is a problem for all Christians, not only Anglicans. Perhaps that means it has no real place in this book. But it insists on a paragraph or so lest our thinking become unrealistic.

The only point at which any Christian dare begin pondering the problem is Christ himself. God became man. That is the Alpha and Omega of indigenization. Christ became incarnate in Palestine and repudiated nothing specifically Palestinian in doing so. (What he repudiated were universals like sin.) The task of the missionary is easily expressed. It is simply to enable Christ in him to become incarnate in Africa or wherever. In doing so he will repudiate nothing specifically African simply because it is African. That means he will not replace African things with European things simply because the African things are African, or because European things are European.

That is the theory. But there is a snag about the practice. Most men, and this includes missionaries, are inescapably (and in many senses, rightly) prisoners of their own culture. My friends, and my enemies too, frequently remind me that I am a Welshman, and their words usually imply that that means I am not an Englishman! Nobody seems able to identify Welshness as against English-ness but the distinction apparently remains no less real. And I remain Welsh.

The missionary cannot but take his own culture with him. The nuances of the Authorized Version of the Bible are inescapable for one who knows only the Authorized Version. What's more, the missionary, inevitably (and in so many ways, rightly) has his own sort of prestige among his children in the Faith. What he has done becomes the model for what converts do; and, doing it, they begin to rationalize it. For example they might say 'Why should we sing Indian music in church? That belongs to Hinduism and we left that behind when we accepted Christ.'

Such things present problems for all missionaries. In so many parts of the world, especially in these days when imperialism is a dirty word, they present especially acute problems for those Anglicans who go from the Church of England. For attempts to distinguish between the faith taught by England's Church and the government imposed by England's State were not always successful. Missionaries spent more time than the cynic might imagine in trying to prove that they were not the secular arm in a Sunday suit. They did not always succeed.

Christian converts were not the only ones affected by this fortuitous Church/State relationship. For Hindus, for instance, the major reason why Anglicanism made an impact on India was because of the British raj. They were convinced that when India gained her independence and the white imperialists were thrown out, the Anglican Church, if not the whole Christian body, would go with them. Well, India is independent and her ecclesiastical organization had quite a shaking up in the process. Yet the Church of the Province is certainly no weaker a decade and a half later. Which is one reason why Hindus, disappointed of their prophecy that Christianity, in general, and Anglicanism, in particular, would retreat with the King-Emperor, are more militantly Hindu than hitherto.

The point which concerns us at the moment is that Anglicans ineluctably have a unique relationship with a specific political and cultural background. This is almost as true of American-based missionaries as it is of those from an English or Dominion background. For, after all, America *was* the first British Empire. And I have a personal impression that they talk about the Magna Carta even more than the English.

This unique relationship with a specific political and cultural background is a frustrating thing to examine. It is easier to say what it is not than what it is. Whatever it is, it probably has some place among the imponderables which link Anglicans, at least historically. Again we must remind ourselves that there are strong Anglican Churches which have had no connection with England's secular imperium. The English background must not be exaggerated even though for our thinking at the moment we dare not minimize it. Its importance cannot be central, or there would not be the sort of Anglican Churches there are in Japan, Korea, Madagascar, Brazil, and other shores where British Imperialism never lapped. Quite obviously, too, any importance it ever had must become progressively more a memory as the British Empire recedes farther back into the pages of the history book. Furthermore, the twentieth-century imperialism centred round Moscow is not likely to give us another case history which would provide any parallels from which we might learn more of the relationships of secular and Christian expansion.

In our musings on the things which bind Anglicans together we have wandered into the realms where things cannot be measured, and detailed observations cannot be scientifically expressed. Is not such a ramble inevitable when you come to express relationships? Can we *scientifically* observe or *logically* analyse the relationship between a father and a child? The reason for our inability lies in the wealth, rather than the poverty, of the relationship.

Nevertheless, there are certain physical facts which can be asserted about any relationship. The Lambeth Conference, for example, is a physical enough fact when you see three hundred and more bishops present in the flesh. We have already noted that no one *invented* the Lambeth Conferences[1] and quite a few bishops resented the first one, violently. That is no longer the case. Indeed, when limitations of space excluded from the 1958 Conference some who were in episcopal orders, there were loud cries of disappointment. These Conferences have become a popular episcopal occasion. They are hardworking parties, a unique forum for the sort of exchange which keeps the lifeblood flowing through the Anglican body.

[1] For a fuller treatment see the author's *The Bishops Come to Lambeth* (1958).

Even here, however, we must have guarded thoughts about the future. It was the 1948 Lambeth Conference which looked forward to the time when there would be 'in every country where there now exists the Anglican Church and others separated from it, a united Church, Catholic and Evangelical, but no longer in the limiting sense of the word Anglican'. That means that the Anglican Communion will have disappeared into something greater than itself. Such, surely, is God's will. But the 1958 Lambeth Conference (rl. 27) had a relevant suggestion: 'There has come before us a vision of a wider fellowship of episcopal Churches finding, if God wills, a focus of unity in the Anglican Communion.'

The Lambeth Conference, of course, can never be fully representative, let alone executive. Nor can its younger brother, the Anglican Congress, the pattern for which was basically worked out at Minneapolis in 1954, to be followed by Toronto in 1963. Open to laity as well as bishops and other clergy, they have a real purpose to serve as a binding force of Anglicanism. They also have many problems to solve before they can do their work properly. Inevitably in a world where the spirit is willing but the economics weak, membership is limited to those who can afford the fare or can get access to a common pool—village pond is a better term—supplied by those who can afford it and appreciate what such a congress can do for the Anglican Communion. For a Congress held in Toronto, access is obviously much easier for the rich and neighbouring diocese of Michigan than for the poor and remote Madagascar or Mauritius. Unlike the secular world, of course, the grievance is not that Michigan, by weight of numbers, can sway decisions. That would not matter, perhaps, even if it were administratively possible, which it is not. It is a sad thing, though, that Madagascar and Mauritius and Meath and Melanesia, and so many other places, should be deprived of the vision and fellowship which such gatherings give.

Another unifying factor in the Anglican Communion is St Augustine's College, Canterbury. It is a point at which the writer's pen gets loaded with fluent ink and evocative adjectives. Set in an incomparable context and atmosphere, it brings together clergy, mature and not so mature, from every corner of the world. There you will find a Dyak from Borneo who always knew of his connection with England, encountering a Filipino, who always knew of his connection with the U.S.A., finding they have a connection with each other in Christ and his Church. St Augustine's, for any visitor, is a living parable of the wealth the nations can bring to each other in Christ. (Like so many Anglican things, wealth in its normal, affluent-society sense is about the last thing which is visible.) Here is something which has all that is needed to fulfil a unique vocation to the glory of God through Anglicanism. All that is needed, except money.

Alongside St Augustine's, Canterbury, must be put its younger brother, St George's College, Jerusalem. By virtue of its site, its associations and so many other things, St Augustine's is right at the heart of Anglicanism, and it helps to warm that heart. To attempt to produce a replica in Jerusalem is indeed a daring statement that Anglicanism has reached the stage where the umbilical cord can safely be severed. Perhaps St George's College is going to prove one of the most significant examples of what Anglicanism, freed of its English context, means.

While thinking of Jerusalem, we might also note a totally improbable episcopate which yet acts as some sort of Anglican bond. The Jerusalem Bishopric was established in 1841 as the result of a strange Anglo-German agreement. It was one of the factors which persuaded John Henry Newman to desert Anglicanism. Its first holder was a Jew. Its present holder is the only Anglican Archbishop without a fully constituted province. Its function is not proselytism, but to make an Anglican contribution to the conversation of the Churches which cluster round the earthly centre of Christianity. What sort of bond for Anglicanism does it make? It is unique, for it is probably the only part of the whole Communion which receives financial support from all the rest of the Communion. It leaves the imagination groping when you read that Anglicans, say, in the tiny Indian Ocean island of Car Nicobar, wholly indigenous, bishop and all, evangelized not by a European but by an Indian, send their Good Friday collections to an Archbishop they will never see, in a land more real to them in the pages of their Bible than in contemporary experience. It seems that a proportionately larger number of Anglicans than of Christians of any other persuasion make a pilgrimage to the Holy Land. Is it because Anglicanism is so Bible-based? Or because Anglicans especially feel there must be something unique about hills and valleys which God honoured in a peculiar way? Is it connected with Anglicanism's emphasis on the Incarnation? Or what?

We come back from speculation to look at another link in this Communion, that glossy magazine, *Anglican World*.[1] It would be out of place for me to suggest, or even imply, that it is the best magazine in the world. But I can speak with some knowledge of the ideals that brought it into existence.

A few Anglicans (interestingly enough the leaders were Welsh, not English) shared the common conviction that until Anglicans know more about each other and become more of a family, God cannot use the Anglican Communion as fully as he wants to. So these Anglicans decided to rush in where angels fear to tread and publish a periodical for which they had no capital. Economically crazy, of course; but anyone who has seen any representative selection of the correspondence which pours into the office will conclude that it is a sanctified form of madness. *Anglican World* exists to help the Anglican Communion become aware of itself and its potentialities. Perhaps that is why someone has christened it 'Stephen Bayne's parish magazine'. It is an apt name . . . and a compliment.

There are two more Anglican links which we have left to the end and both are vital. They are personal, and we hesitate to

[1]Editor: The Rev. Peter Harvey, 29 Tufton Street, London, S.W.1.

write about them because both are modest and, if the world would let them be, retiring persons. One is the Archbishop of Canterbury, the other is the Executive Officer of the Anglican Communion.

There have been a hundred Archbishops of Canterbury and each one has been a different person. In other words, there is no single image. By the strict letter of the law, the Archbishop of Canterbury possesses little authority outside his own diocese, and practically none outside his own province. Apart from a few missionary dioceses, which are constantly being reduced in number as new independent provinces are formed, he has no jurisdiction outside England. An Archbishop of Canterbury, for example, has no sort of authority in Wales, except he be invited. The Archbishop of Canterbury lacks the *mystique* which attaches to the Pope, and he certainly lacks any claim to infallibility. What he does have is the sort of respect accorded to a father by a grown up family of fully emancipated sons. While that respect may spring from filial relationships, it has to be earned if it is to be retained. The fact is, of course, that the great Archbishops of Canterbury have earned it, and the office has acquired a prestige not so much by any regulations or agreements, formal or informal, as by the character of the holders. There is one noticeable fact. The Archbishop of Canterbury is usually a much greater man when he lays down his duties than when he takes them up. He somehow demonstrates a capacity to grow to the size of the job. If there can be pragmatic proofs that the Holy Spirit is given in such a measure as a man needs and accepts, this is such proof. The same Holy Spirit who does such mysterious things through the Anglican Communion does mysterious things with its father-figure. The Archbishop of Canterbury thus helps build the whole family more closely together. We must have no illusions, however, about the father-figure becoming a *papa*. There is no papal image here. The Archbishop of Canterbury remains the head of the Anglican family only as long as he is prepared to renounce all paternal authority. When the family gathers in his house he is head of the table. But the selection of what is on the table is very much a matter for all.

Which brings us to the Anglican Executive Officer, the Secretary to the Advisory Council for Missionary Strategy, and the Secretary to the Consultative Body of the Lambeth Conference. Three offices—one officer (who happens to have sundry other duties, such as care of American Anglicans in Europe, as makeweight).

In 1960, Bishop Stephen F. Bayne descended from the heights of Olympia (his diocese in the U.S.A.) and began to go to and fro in the earth among the sons of men. 'This officer,' said the 1958 Lambeth Conference with gay insouciance (p. II. 70), 'would collect and disseminate information, keep open lines of communication and make contact when necessary with responsible authority.' Those eloquent—grandiloquent?—words boil down to a house in London called Compasrose and an annual travel schedule that makes Marco Polo seem static. And what is this episcopal pilgrim doing?

That, in a sense, is what this book is all about, and if we could answer that last question in one short formula, there would be no need for the book. On the other hand, if we began by talking in any detail about the sort of job he is doing, it would double the length of this book and even the most forbearing reader has a limit to his patience.

But there is an observation which insists on getting on to paper. The Executive Officer is himself a parable of Anglicanism. When the Lambeth Conference felt the time had come to create a new office to help Anglicanism become more aware of itself, and thus more capable of being used by God, it did not evolve a long constitution of rules and regulations for the job; nor did it produce any clearly delineated terms of reference; nor did it start by putting down on paper any details of an imposing organization. It just decided to appoint a person, and the lot fell on Stephen Bayne.

It appointed a *person*; and thereby, possibly unconsciously, proclaimed that the Christian Faith is ultimately not a matter of persons and of the relationship between persons and the Person. It is a relationship that saints and sages down the centuries have tried to express in words, and valiant have been the attempts. But in the end even the most eloquent fall silent and share the wistfulness of St John when he supposed that even the world itself could not contain the books that should be written if all the mysteries of God could be reduced to ink and paper.

Anglicanism deeply, albeit dimly, realizes that the man-to-God-to-men relationship wings far beyond any analysis and definition. That, perhaps, is the reason why 'Anglican spirituality' is a phrase which has acquired a rich cargo of meaning. Anglicans who keep on pleading that they be allowed to express their beliefs in worship rather than in doctrinal theses have somewhere along the line found a whole climate of spiritual attitudes and values, and it is a bond between them because it is primarily a bond between them and God. 'Theology always issues in doxology when it is true to its theme,' says Canon Kenneth Cragg.[1] Doxology is the eternal function which neither life nor death, nor all the principalities nor all the powers can prevent. It is man's ultimate freedom—and a freedom which comes from his recognition of ultimate authority.

Is doxology itself a matter of words? Is it no more than finding adjectives and attributes with which we can tell God what we think of him? By no means. It also involves the way of life which is consistent with the presence of majesty, which is responsive to the infinitude of mercy, which sees all men as the object of the divine love and therefore as the subjects of one's own love. Above all, doxology is the free but fearful use of the Body and Blood which were given on Calvary and are given on each altar. Here we have reached the core of what binds Anglicans together. It is a core so radiant that the eyes are dazzled and the lips fall silent.

Yet one fact must be stated plainly, if only because it is so

[1] *Call of the Minaret* (1956), p. 66.

obvious a fact that it might get lost through familiarity. All this diversity of Anglicanism, as multiform and variegated as humanity itself, becomes one as each, entering into full communion with his Lord, whose remembrance is a Presence, attains full communion with each other. In this the most ill-provided Asian peasant woman becomes one with the Queen of England, and the humblest ordained African shares the same priesthood as the Archbishop of Canterbury. Thus is one membership in one Lord, one Faith, one Baptism shared by multifarious peoples divided by a thousand earthly barriers. And the picture of a heavenly, but still pilgrim host begins to develop from the negative of sinful men.

God grant that we who are called to draw this pattern of light and darkness may one day become worthy of our glimpse of his love, and that our light may so shine before men, all men, that they may glorify their Father and ours!

For that, after all, is our final, all-embracing agenda.

Epilogue

THIS HAS been a book of questions rather than of answers. It might be helpful if we tried to crystallize those questions into a few pages. But a very clear *caveat* is first called for: let no one imagine that this book carries any authority, official or unofficial. Neither S.P.G. on whose staff I have been working, nor any of those I delight to call friends, can be held responsible. No one has given the author a mandate to set the course of the Anglican Communion. All he has is what everyone has: the duty of asking why God has placed him in the particular situation in which he finds himself. He asks, too, the question which is its corollary: what would he do if, by some unhappy error, he were called to plan the agenda for a meeting of Anglican Archbishops and other metropolitans.

The first thing he would try to do would be to realize that the primary duty of each metropolitan is towards that particular part of the flock of which he has been made Chief Shepherd. No one has the right to think and plan for the whole Communion if it is to be at the expense of his own especial responsibility. But it is hard to believe that in the long run there is any conflict between the real welfare of a part and the welfare of the whole.

The second thing would be to try to define the areas which call for action, aware that each overlaps the other and ultimately all are one. There appear to be four such areas in which each Anglican Church should ponder its life and work:

    (i) towards God

    (ii) towards non-Anglican Churches

    (iii) towards other Anglican Churches

    (iv) towards the 'secular' world.

Since this book is concerned with peculiarly Anglican problems, responsibility towards the 'secular' world need not take our time here (even though it must be a constant concern everywhere). For it is a question which must lie equally on the minds of every baptized Christian, of whatever affiliation. Thus, for example, in the continuing debate on the Church's approach to industrialization there are not likely to be specifically *Anglican* insights—though specific Anglicans, we trust, can make particular contributions. Number four must be the concern of all Christendom.

So, too, must the first question. But if the Anglican emphasis on *lex orandi, lex credendi* is true and valid there must be a particular Anglican approach to its forms of worship. The way Anglicans speak about their relationship must be accompanied by a willingness to struggle towards some sort of common mind about Prayer Book revision and this common mind must be sufficiently strong and sensitive to influence the Prayer Book revisings of each Anglican Church. We must recognize that the very revising of the Prayer Book, if carried out by one province in total isolation from its fellows, can impede Anglican unity. As one who, for the time being at least, lives in the Church of England I am deeply aware of how much the English Prayer Book can learn from its sisters. But I am also aware of how indifferent to the experience and knowledge of others Prayer Book revisers can be. If the Prayer Book is important it is no less important for the best brains to ponder its place and potentiality in the Anglican Communion and its function as part of Anglican relationships.

Closely allied to the mode of worship is the content of prayer. Again there is an Anglican inadequacy. At the moment, however dire the need of an Anglican province for the prayers of the rest of the family on some occasion, it has no very clear means of communicating the fact. Here, surely, is a point at which the need for inter-Anglican communication is evident. But how?

Moving from the Anglican duty towards God we would next ask metropolitans to consider the Anglican duty towards non-Anglican Churches. How can Anglicans get closer to a common mind in their dealings with other Churches? If, for example, any Anglican diocese wants to know the thoughts of its fellows about some local reunion scheme, how can it avoid getting the confusion of conflict and compromise which seems to be the present likeliest risk? And this risk must continue as long as each province makes its own judgements practically in isolation from its fellows. And how, when assembled in ecumenical conclave, can other Churches be assured they are getting a really representative Anglican contribution rather than the—no doubt sincere—personal opinion of someone who just happens to be present?

Again, in those things which Anglicans look forward to receiving *from* other Churches how are they to ensure that a gift one province has received will become the privilege of all?

Then, in regard to the relationship of each Anglican Church to all its fellows: the metropolitans must surely consider whether we are to continue to face the manifest dangers of being an adult family where everyone is so equal that no one is able to call the others together for practical *working* parties, to implement the undoubtedly high quality *thinking* parties which are a Lambeth Conference or an Anglican Congress. How are Anglicans to embark on the real, intimate and practical dialogue about their common task? There are so many areas in which this dialogue is called for. One, particularly, both demonstrates the need and presents perhaps the most hopeful chance of a really practical experiment. It is the fulfilment of the Mission. In terms of mission administration each province, at least among the 'older' Churches, probably already has a more highly developed organization than it has in any other field. Furthermore, there can be no question of the duty of the Anglican Communion to deploy its forces of prayer, men, women and money to the very best advantage—which it is some way from doing at the moment. Is it not possible to make a beginning by asking the Mission organization or organizations in each province to struggle to find how the various strengths and weaknesses can be better related? It is worth remembering that the International Missionary Council not only preceded but also helped point the way to the World Council of Churches. Has the time come for an Inter-Anglican Missionary Council, consisting largely of missionary organization staff, so that we really can discover, for example, what the Church of England can learn about mission organization from the Episcopal Church in the U.S.A., or we can begin to ascertain whether the Church, say, in Australia lacks some category of missionary which the Church in Canada may have in abundance?

If Anglican Churches can once begin to learn from each other in one field the way will be pointed towards learning in many others—evangelism, stewardship, the retreat movement, Christian literature, synodical or other forms of government— there is plenty of room for action. And the more we act together the nearer we shall come to a common mind.

In facing the problems of attaining a common mind in their approach towards God, their approach towards non-Anglican Churches and their approach to each other, the metropolitans will need to keep asking themselves just what is the significance of 'John to the seven Churches which are in Asia'. What are the validity, the meaning, the function, the relationships of a National Church in the shrinking world of the twentieth century? What is the connection between independence and inter-dependence, between being autonomous and mature and being a member of a family where all are equal?

Today this problem of the meaning of national or regional Churches reaches its most acute form in the relationship of missionary organizations with 'receiving' Churches. That is something which, day by day, simply has to be worked out in practice. Sometimes the agony is very real. God is surely teaching us something through such travail. But the lesson is as yet barely begun.

And, perhaps most important of all, the metropolitans will ask themselves just how to explore further and use still better that Anglican counterpoint between freedom and authority which is an inescapable mark of this Communion.

There is one last question this book must ask itself. Have we laid ourselves open to a charge of Pelagianism—perhaps a peculiarly British heresy? Have we implied that unless *we* can get things properly organized and detailed, God will not be able to act? Have we forgotten the Holy Spirit who blows where he lists? We pray this is not the case.

One of the most acute moments of all the earthly ministry of Jesus came when, in the wilderness, he was tempted of the Devil. 'Jump down from the top of the Temple,' he was told, 'Leave it to God to look after you! He will see everything works out all right!' And in simple, searing words, Jesus pointed out that God expects our co-operation and our common sense. 'Thou shalt not tempt the Lord thy God.'

Are Anglicans tempting God? Are they just ambling carelessly on in a world-wide family which came into being by no human plan and thereby neglecting responsibilities which God has laid upon them?

This book does not know the answer to that question. It has been written in the hope that others wiser and more perceptive will continue to ask it and to pray:

'O God, why hast thou made this Anglican Communion? *For Christ's sake*, tell us. Amen.'